THE ESSENCE OF TAIJI QIGONG

Painted by Chow, Chian-Chiu (周千秋)

Text:

It is said that the Song Daoist Zhang, San-Feng, after he saw the way a crane and a snake fought, created Taijiquan, which is effective for sickness prevention and longevity. I have practiced Taiji for many decades and have verified this saying.

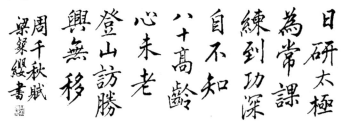

I study Taiji everyday as a regular lesson
I have achieved the deep Gongfu, though I didn't realize it
At the age of eighty, my heart is not yet old
Climbing mountains and visiting well-known scenes have
never lost my interest

Poetry by Chow, Chian-Chiu (周千秋)
Calligraphy by Leung, Chen-Ying (梁粲纓)
Translation by Dr. Yang, Jwing-Ming (楊俊敏)

The Essence of Taiji Qigong

太極氣功

-The Internal Foundation of Taijiquan-

YMAA Publication Center
Boston, Mass. USA

YMAA Publication Center
Main Office:
  PO Box 480
  Wolfeboro, NH 03894
  1-800-669-8892 • www.ymaa.com • ymaa@aol.com

ISBN-10: 1-886969-63-9
ISBN-13: 978-1-886969-63-6

POD0910

Publisher's Cataloging-in-Publication
(Provided by Quality Books, Inc.)

Yang, Jwing-Ming 1946-
    The essence of taiji qigong : the internal foundation of
taijiquan / Jwing-Ming Yang.—2nd ed.
    p. cm. —(Martial arts—qigong)
    Includes bibiographical references and index.
    Preassigned LCCN: 98-60108
    ISBN: 978-1-59439-111-8

    1. Ch'i kung. 2. T'ai chi ch'uan. 3. Martial arts. 4.
Alternative medicine. I. Title. II. Series.

RA 781.8.Y36 1998   613.7'14'8
                           QBI98-667

Figures 2-4, 3-33, 3-34, 3-35, 3-36, 3-37, 3-38, 3-40, and 3-41 modified by Sarah Noack.
Original images copyright ©1994 by TechPool Studios Corp. USA, 1463 Warrensville Center Road,
Cleveland, OH 44121.

Disclaimer:
The author and publisher of this material are NOT RESPONSIBLE in any manner whatsoever for any
injury which may occur through reading or following the instructions in this manual.
The activities, physical or otherwise, described in this material may be too strenuous or dangerous for
some people, and the reader(s) should consult a physician before engaging in them.

Acknowledgments for the First Edition

Thanks to A. Reza Farman-Farmaian for the photography, Wen-Ching Wu for the drawings, Michael Wiederhold for the typesetting, and John R. Redmond for the cover drawing. Thanks also to David Ripianzi, Roger Whidden Jr., James O'Leary, Jr., and many other YMAA members for proofing the manuscript and for contributing many valuable suggestions and discussions. Special thanks to Alan Dougall for his editing. And a very special thanks to the artists Chow, Chian-Chiu and Leung, Chen-Ying for their beautiful painting and calligraphy on the frontispiece of this book.

Acknowledgments for the Second Edition

In this new edition, I would like to express many thanks to Tim Comrie for his typesetting and general help and to Erik Elsemans for proofing the manuscript. Special thanks to James O'Leary for his editing, Ilana Rosenberg for her cover design, and to David Zaboski for the cover concept—Approaching Wuji from Taiji.

Romanization of Chinese Words

This book uses the Pinyin romanization system of Chinese to English. Pinyin is standard in the People's Republic of China, and in several world organizations, including the United Nations. Pinyin, which was introduced in China in the 1950's, replaces the Wade-Giles and Yale systems. In some cases, the more popular spelling of a word may be used for clarity.

Some common conversions:

Pinyin	Also Spelled As	Pronunciation
Qi	Chi	chē
Qigong	Chi Kung	chē kŭng
Qin Na	Chin Na	chĭn nă
Jin	Jing	jĭn
Gongfu	Kung Fu	gŏng foo
Taijiquan	Tai Chi Chuan	tī jē chŭén

For more information, please refer to *The People's Republic of China: Administrative Atlas, The Reform of the Chinese Written Language,* or a contemporary manual of style.

Contents

About the Author

Dr. Yang, Jwing-Ming, Ph.D.

楊俊敏博士

Dr. Yang, Jwing-Ming was born on August 11, 1946, in Xinzhu Xian (新竹縣), Taiwan (台灣), Republic of China (中華民國). He started his Wushu (武術)(Gongfu or Kung Fu, 功夫) training at the age of fifteen under the Shaolin White Crane (Bai He, 少林白鶴) Master Cheng, Gin-Gsao (曾金灶). Master Cheng originally learned Taizuquan (太祖拳) from his grandfather when he was a child. When Master Cheng was fifteen years old, he started learning White Crane from Master Jin, Shao-Feng (金紹峰), and followed him for twenty-three years until Master Jin's death.

In thirteen years of study (1961-1974 A.D.) under Master Cheng, Dr. Yang became an expert in the White Crane Style of Chinese martial arts, which includes both the use of barehands and of various weapons such as saber, staff, spear, trident, two short rods, and many other weapons. With the same master he also studied White Crane Qigong (氣功), Qin Na (or Chin Na, 擒拿), Tui Na (推拿) and Dian Xue massages (點穴按摩), and herbal treatment.

At the age of sixteen, Dr. Yang began the study of Yang Style Taijiquan (楊氏太極拳) under Master Kao Tao (高濤). After learning from Master Kao, Dr. Yang continued his study and research of Taijiquan with several masters and senior practitioners such as Master Li, Mao-Ching (李茂清) and Mr. Wilson Chen (陳威伸) in Taipei (台北). Master Li learned his Taijiquan from the well-known Master Han, Ching-Tang (韓慶堂), and Mr. Chen learned his Taijiquan from Master Chang, Xiang-San (張祥三). Dr. Yang has mastered the Taiji barehand sequence, pushing hands, the two-man fighting sequence, Taiji sword, Taiji saber, and Taiji Qigong.

When Dr. Yang was eighteen years old, he entered Tamkang University (淡江學院) in Taipei Xian to study Physics. In college he began the study of traditional Shaolin Long Fist (Changquan or Chang Chuan, 少林長拳) with Master Li, Mao-Ching at the Tamkang College Guoshu Club (淡江國術社)(1964-1968 A.D.), and eventually became an assistant instructor under Master Li. In 1971 he completed his M.S. degree in Physics at the National Taiwan University (台灣大學), and then served in the Chinese Air Force from 1971 to 1972. In the service, Dr. Yang taught Physics at the Junior Academy of the Chinese Air Force (空軍幼校) while also teaching Wushu. After being honorably discharged in 1972, he returned to Tamkang College to teach Physics and resumed study under Master Li, Mao-Ching. From Master Li, Dr. Yang learned Northern Style Wushu, which includes both barehand (especially kicking) techniques and numerous weapons.

In 1974, Dr. Yang came to the United States to study Mechanical Engineering at Purdue University. At the request of a few students, Dr. Yang began to teach Gongfu (Kung Fu), which resulted in the foundation of the Purdue University Chinese Kung Fu Research Club in the spring of 1975. While at Purdue, Dr. Yang also taught college-credited courses in Taijiquan. In

May of 1978 he was awarded a Ph.D. in Mechanical Engineering by Purdue.

In 1980, Dr. Yang moved to Houston to work for Texas Instruments. While in Houston he founded Yang's Shaolin Kung Fu Academy, which was eventually taken over by his disciple Mr. Jeffery Bolt after he moved to Boston in 1982. Dr. Yang founded Yang's Martial Arts Academy (YMAA) in Boston on October 1, 1982.

In January of 1984 he gave up his engineering career to devote more time to research, writing, and teaching. In March of 1986 he purchased property in the Jamaica Plain area of Boston to be used as the headquarters of the new organization, Yang's Martial Arts Association. The organization has continued to expand, and, as of July 1, 1989, YMAA has become just one division of Yang's Oriental Arts Association, Inc. (YOAA, Inc.).

In summary, Dr. Yang has been involved in Chinese Wushu since 1961. During this time, he has spent thirteen years learning Shaolin White Crane (Bai He), Shaolin Long Fist (Changquan), and Taijiquan. Dr. Yang has more than twenty-nine years of instructional experience: seven years in Taiwan, five years at Purdue University, two years in Houston, Texas, and fifteen years in Boston, Massachusetts.

In addition, Dr. Yang has also been invited to offer seminars around the world to share his knowledge of Chinese martial arts and Qigong. The countries he has visited include Canada, Mexico, France, Italy, Poland, England, Ireland, Portugal, Switzerland, Germany, Hungary, Spain, Holland, Latvia, South Africa, and Saudi Arabia.

Since 1986, YMAA has become an international organization, which currently includes thirty-seven schools located in Poland, Portugal, France, Switzerland, Italy, Ireland, Holland, Hungary, Belgium, South Africa, the United Kingdom, Canada, and the United States. Many of Dr. Yang's books and videotapes have been translated into languages such as French, Italian, Spanish, Polish, Czech, Bulgarian, Dutch, Russian, and Hungarian.

Dr. Yang has written twenty-two volumes on the martial arts and Qigong:

1. *Shaolin Chin Na;* Unique Publications, Inc., 1980.
2. *Shaolin Long Fist Kung Fu;* Unique Publications, Inc., 1981.
3. *Yang Style Tai Chi Chuan;* Unique Publications, Inc., 1981.
4. *Introduction to Ancient Chinese Weapons;* Unique Publications, Inc.,1985.
5. *Qigong for Health and Martial Arts;* YMAA Publication Center, 1985.
6. *Northern Shaolin Sword;* YMAA Publication Center, 1985.
7. *Tai Chi Theory and Martial Power;* YMAA Publication Center, 1986.
8. *Tai Chi Chuan Martial Applications,* YMAA Publication Center, 1986.

9. *Analysis of Shaolin Chin Na;* YMAA Publication Center, 1987.

10. *Eight Simple Qigong Exercises for Health;* YMAA Publication Center, 1988.

11. *The Root of Chinese Qigong—The Secrets of Qigong Training;* YMAA Publication Center, 1989.

12. *Muscle/Tendon Changing and Marrow/Brain Washing Chi Kung—The Secret of Youth;* YMAA Publication Center, 1989.

13. *Hsing Yi Chuan—Theory and Applications;* YMAA Publication Center, 1990.

14. *The Essence of Taiji Qigong—Health and Martial Arts;* YMAA Publication Center, 1990.

15. *Qigong for Arthritis;* YMAA Publication Center, 1991.

16. *Chinese Qigong Massage—General Massage;* YMAA Publication Center, 1992.

17. *How to Defend Yourself;* YMAA Publication Center, 1992.

18. *Baguazhang—Emei Baguazhang;* YMAA Publication Center, 1994.

19. *Comprehensive Applications of Shaolin Chin Na—The Practical Defense of Chinese Seizing Arts;* YMAA Publication Center, 1995.

20. *Taiji Chin Na—The Seizing Art of Taijiquan;* YMAA Publication Center, 1995.

21. *The Essence of Shaolin White Crane;* YMAA Publication Center, 1996.

22. *Back Pain—Chinese Qigong for Healing & Prevention;* YMAA Publication Center, 1997.

Dr. Yang has also produced the following videotapes:

1. *Yang Style Tai Chi Chuan and Its Applications;* YMAA Publication Center, 1984.

2. *Shaolin Long Fist Kung Fu—Lien Bu Chuan and Its Applications;* YMAA Publication Center, 1985.

3. *Shaolin Long Fist Kung Fu—Gung Li Chuan and Its Applications;* YMAA Publication Center, 1986.

4. *Shaolin Chin Na;* YMAA Publication Center, 1987.

5. *Wai Dan Chi Kung, Vol. 1—The Eight Pieces of Brocade;* YMAA Publication Center, 1987.

6. *Chi Kung for Tai Chi Chuan;* YMAA Publication Center, 1990.

7. *Qigong for Arthritis;* YMAA Publication Center, 1991.

8. *Qigong Massage—Self Massage;* YMAA Publication Center, 1992.

9. *Qigong Massage—With a Partner;* YMAA Publication Center, 1992.

10. *Defend Yourself 1—Unarmed Attack;* YMAA Publication Center, 1992.

11. *Defend Yourself 2—Knife Attack;* YMAA Publication Center, 1992.

12. *Comprehensive Applications of Shaolin Chin Na 1;* YMAA Publication Center, 1995.

13. *Comprehensive Applications of Shaolin Chin Na 2;* YMAA Publication Center, 1995.

14. *Shaolin Long Fist Kung Fu—Yi Lu Mai Fu & Er Lu Mai Fu;* YMAA Publication Center, 1995.

15. *Shaolin Long Fist Kung Fu—Shi Zi Tang;* YMAA Publication Center, 1995.

16. *Taiji Chin Na;* YMAA Publication Center, 1995.

17. *Emei Baguazhang—1; Basic Training, Qigong, Eight Palms, and Applications;* YMAA Publication Center, 1995.

18. *Emei Baguazhang—2; Swimming Body Baguazhang and Its Applications;* YMAA Publication Center, 1995.

19. *Emei Baguazhang—3; Bagua Deer Hook Sword and Its Applications;* YMAA Publication Center, 1995.

20. *Xingyiquan—12 Animal Patterns and Their Applications;* YMAA Publication Center, 1995.

21. *Simplified Tai Chi Chuan—Simplified 24 Postures & Standard 48 Postures;* YMAA Publication Center, 1995.

22. *Tai Chi Chuan & Applications—Simplified 24 Postures with Applications & Standard 48 Postures;* YMAA Publication Center, 1995.

23. *White Crane Hard Qigong;* YMAA Publication Center, 1997.

24. *White Crane Soft Qigong;* YMAA Publication Center, 1997.

25. *Xiao Hu Yan—Intermediate Level Long Fist Sequence;* YMAA Publication Center, 1997.

26. *Back Pain—Chinese Qigong for Healing and Prevention;* YMAA Publication Center, 1997.

27. *The Scientific Foundation of Chinese Qigong;* YMAA Publication Center, 1997.

Foreword

In the past few years, the general populace of the U.S. has been facing a radical reexamination of the state of our health care system. Not only has this investigation included wide-ranging debates on how health care is delivered and who pays the bills, it also has brought us to a different vantage point for examining our philosophical approach to health and well-being. We have been forced to reexamine our involvement in our own health care by the realizations that many new diseases and dysfunctions are rising up to challenge us, and that the world has become so closely connected that what affects people on one continent will soon be active throughout the global village. Swiftly we made the discovery that we must be responsible for our own state of health; we have understood that we are either our own best friend or our own worst enemy when it comes to caring for ourselves. The requirement that we care for ourselves—selfcare—has brought us to a need for effective methods of regaining or maintaining our state of well-being.

We have been turning to what was first called "alternative" health practices and then soon termed "complementary" health practices. These changes in our approach are not due to the lack of skills among contemporary medicine practitioners nor to dearth of research and empirical proofs. Never have we had better medicines, machines, and methods, nor better proof of their effectiveness. Modern medicine has not failed us; the state of medical research and care and research has never been higher. Why then are so many people unhealthy? What has happened is that we allowed ourselves to become dependent upon someone else or something else to "fix" our ailments, our bodies, our lives. These repairs have accomplished much, but too often they are not complete or not permanent. As we look around us for models of good health, we see that people who are bright, energetic, stress-free, happy—in short, healthy—are those who take care of themselves, and we ask what they are doing that makes them healthy and keeps them in that state.

People who take care of their health care for themselves in all areas—physical, mental, emotional, psychological, and spiritual—and those who have the best success in those regards, have discovered methods that care for all aspects at the same time. What they have discovered is the catalyst that makes all health care really work: the realization of the wholeness of our being. Many people have been fortunate enough to discover the traditional oriental exercise and practices that emphasize the development of these connections: the practices of Qigong and Taiji.

Until very recently, few people had heard of either of these, but over the past decade much information has come to light and been documented in terms that make research results acceptable in our culture, and now nearly everyone knows at least a little about them. In this light, it is important that, as we turn to ancient and little known forms of health practice, we have a contemporary and thorough guide.

Dr. Yang is the best possible person to be this guide. His own credentials are well documented, and as a member of the faculty of A Taste of China for many years, he has consistently been very well received by students as he presented information on a variety of topics associated with Chinese health practices in general, and Taijiquan and Qigong specifically. As director of A Taste of China, an organization which since 1983 has promoted Chinese martial arts in general and presented international seminars, and national and international tournaments, I have been pleased to include Dr. Yang as one of our most popular presenters. His depth of knowledge and his superb teaching style make him among the most valuable members of this community.

His background and training are very suitable to the subject of internal development, combining personal experience with a scholarly approach. He is able to present the setting and history of Qigong and Taiji without overemphasizing the relationship of background to the actual practices. He uses terms that have been in place for centuries and brings them into current usage, and he includes the right amount of information to acquaint us with the concepts. It's the mark of a cultured person to be able to combine the ancient with the modern, the esoteric with the common, the physical with the mental, and the theory with the practice, and Dr. Yang does these brilliantly.

His style of explaining makes the information accessible; the personal touch of addressing the reader directly involves us in the process he is describing, stimulates interest, and reassures us that we can accomplish these exercises and achieve the desired results. It's "user friendly" in the same way that directions are effectively given for accessing information from other sources, that is, with clean outlines, plain language, clearly marked cautions, and complete illustrations. His teaching style matches his writing and literary style; simple, direct, thorough. He has respect for his readers but makes no assumptions about our level of expertise, and he speaks to us neither over our heads nor beneath our dignity. In this book, as in his others, he has developed a style that explains as clearly as possible in the medium of print and paper what you are supposed to do and feel, and why.

As we rediscover our bodies and our minds and make the connections that were always there to be made, it is important to have this resource, whose greatest value is that it leads us gently and effectively in the right way of practice and understanding, and that it helps us achieve our goal of health and well-being.

Pat Rice
Director, A Taste of China
Winchester, Virginia
July 10, 1998

Preface—First Edition

In the last twenty years, the Chinese concept of "Qi" has gradually come to be understood by the Western public and accepted by modern medical society. It is now believed that Qi is the "bioelectricity" circulating in the human body. It is only in the last twenty years that the field of bioelectricity has gradually opened up in modern science. Because of the interest in this new field of study, and also because of the more open communication with Chinese culture, this field will probably bloom in the next twenty years. The most obvious indications of this are the widespread acceptance of acupuncture treatment for illness and the popularity of Qigong and Taijiquan.

Surprisingly, the main reason for the popularity of Taijiquan is not its martial potential, but rather its ability to improve health. Although it is a martial art, Taijiquan brings the practitioner to a high level of body relaxation, calmness, and peace of mind. Most important of all, it improves the internal Qi circulation, which is the key to maintaining health and curing many illnesses.

Unlike other internal martial styles such as Xingyiquan, Bagua, and Liu He Ba Fa, the beginning training of Taijiquan is completely relaxed and the use of the muscles is reduced to a minimum. Because of this, it can be practiced by people of all ages. According to my personal teaching experience, a large percentage of people beginning Taiji are ill or elderly. Especially in China, Taiji is well known for its ability to improve or even cure many illnesses, notably problems of the stomach, lungs, heart, kidneys, high blood pressure, arthritis, mental disorders, and many others. Once you understand the principles of Qigong and Taiji training theory, you will be able to understand how this can be.

Although Taijiquan can give you a relaxed body and a calm mind, the most important benefit you can gain is a higher level of understanding of life and nature. Taiji leads you to the path by which you can use energy to communicate with nature. This is the path to both physical health and mental or spiritual health. Once you have achieved this, how can you wonder about or be unsure of the meaning of life?

The Qigong sets used in Taijiquan are simple exercises which give you a feeling for your Qi, and start you on the road to understanding how to work with your Qi. It does not just improve your Qi circulation, it is the key to the successful practice of Taijiquan for either health or martial purposes. In fact, there is not much difference between Taiji Qigong and Taijiquan itself. All of the requirements for correct practice are exactly the same for both of them. The only difference is that the Qigong forms are much simpler than the Taijiquan movements. This allows the practitioner to concentrate all of his effort on improving his ability to feel inside his body. Some of the forms in the Qigong sets are actually simplified movements adapted from the Taijiquan sequence.

There are a number of different styles of Taijiquan, each with their own Qigong sets. In this book I will introduce the ones which have been passed down to me from my masters. The first chapter will review the historical background of Qigong and Taijiquan, and introduce the general theoretical and training concepts of Qigong. The second chapter will discuss the root or essence of the Taiji training theory: Yin and Yang. Finally, the third chapter will introduce the Taiji Qigong exercises.

Dr. Yang, Jwing-Ming
Boston, 1993

Preface—Second Edition

Since Chinese acupuncture was introduced to the West, the concept of Qi and its circulation in the human body has gained recognition and acceptance from both physicians and the public. More and more people in this country are turning to acupuncture treatments or trying Qigong to improve their health. As they gain knowledge and experience the wonderful benefits of their practice, the reputation of these Oriental arts increases.

Practicing Qigong (which is the science of working with Qi, the living energy within the body) can not only enhance your health and mental balance, but can also cure a number of illnesses, decreasing the need for medicines and drugs. Qigong uses both still and moving meditation to increase and regulate the Qi circulation.

When you practice regularly, your mind will gradually grow calm and peaceful, and your whole being will start to feel more balanced. However, the most important result of regular Qigong practice is the discovery of the inner world of your body's energy. Through sensing, feeling and examining your inner experiences, you will begin to understand yourself not only physically, but also mentally and energetically. This science of internal sensing, which the Chinese have been studying for hundreds of years, is mostly ignored in the West. However, in today's busy and confusing society, this training is especially vital. With the peace, calmness and energetic smoothness that Qigong can provide, you will be better able to relax and enjoy your daily work, and perhaps even find real happiness.

I believe that it is very important for the West to learn, study, research, and develop this scientific internal art immediately and on a wide scale. I believe that it can be very effective in helping people, especially young people, to cope with the confusing and frightening challenges of life. The general practice of Qigong balances the inner energy of our lives, and can be both healing and instructive to its practitioners. Older people especially will find that it will maintain their health and even slow the aging process, as well as maintaining a healthy body. In addition, Qigong can help older people to conquer depression, and improve their quality of life. I am confident that people in the West will realize that Qigong practice will give them a new perspective on themselves and the universe of energy which they both create and inhabit.

During the last thirteen years, I have traveled all over the world to share my knowledge of Qigong and Chinese martial arts. One of the "hot" subjects that I am frequently asked about is Taiji Qigong. Through Taiji Qigong practice, countless Taijiquan practitioners have had their eyes opened to the inner feeling of Qi, and have learned how to balance and manipulate it creatively and constructively. From this feeling and understanding, these practitioners learn how to adopt Taijiquan practice into their daily lives both physically and mentally. This is because Taiji Qigong is the foundation of Taijiquan practice. Once you comprehend this and can access the deep feeling of this foundation, your Taijiquan practice will evolve into a deeper and more profound art.

I am very happy to see this new version of *The Essence of Taiji Qigong* become available to the public. Other than correcting some minor errors found in the earlier edition, I have also changed all of the Chinese spelling into the Pinyin system, which has become more popular both in laymen and academic circles.

After you have read this book, if you find yourself interested in knowing more about Chinese Qigong, you may refer to other books I have written on this subject.

Beginner Level:
1. *Qigong for Health and Martial Arts*
2. *Eight Simple Qigong Exercises for Health* (Special Qigong style)
3. *Arthritis—The Chinese Way of Healing and Prevention* (Special Qigong treatment)
4. *Back Pain—Chinese Qigong for Healing and Prevention* (Special Qigong treatment)

Intermediate Level:
1. *Qigong Massage—General Massage*

Advanced Level:
1. *The Root of Chinese Qigong*
2. *Muscle/Tendon Changing and Marrow/Brain Washing Chi Kung*
3. *The Essence of Shaolin White Crane*

Companion videotapes are also available for many of the above publications. You may obtain a free catalog from YMAA Publication Center.

Dr. Yang, Jwing-Ming
Boston, January 7, 1998

CHAPTER 1

General Introduction

一般介紹

1.1 Introduction

Qigong, the study of the energy in the universe, is one of the great cultural achievements that China has contributed to the human race. It was through the study of Qi that the balance between the Yin (陰) and Yang (陽) aspects of the universe was understood. This understanding led to the formulation of the "Dao" (道)(the natural way, pronounced "Da-oh"), which became one of the guiding principles of Chinese philosophy. This "Dao" has come to be used in explaining not only nature, but also mankind. The Chinese hope that the study of the Dao can demonstrate the way to improve health or even to extend life. This led to the development of Chinese medicine. The circulation of Qi in the body was also studied, which became the field of human Qigong.

According to Chinese medical theory, the Qi or energy body is considered Yin, while the physical body is considered Yang. Qi cannot be seen, but it can be felt. The Yin aspect of your body is related to your thinking, soul, and spirit, while the Yang aspect executes and experiences the decisions of the Yin. Neither part can survive by itself. They must balance and coordinate with each other so that life can exist. Qi is the source of life, and the actions of the physical body are the manifestation of life. When the Yin is strong, the manifestation of Yang can also be strong. When Yin is weak or too strong, the Yin and Yang may lose balance and

1

sickness can result. For this reason, Chinese medicine and Qigong are primarily concerned with how to maintain the correct balance of Yin and Yang.

According to many documents, although many other cultures have discovered the circulation of Qi, none of them have studied it as deeply as the Chinese. It was only in the last twenty years that the West has begun to accept the concept of Qi, equating it with the bioelectricity circulating in the human body. More and more, Western doctors are starting to recognize that abnormal or irregular Qi or bioelectric circulation is one of the main causes of physical and mental illnesses. Many Western physicians are sending patients to acupuncturists for an alternative method of treatment for certain diseases that Western medicine has difficulty treating. Some are even encouraging patients to take up Qigong or Taiji as a means of enhancing their health and quality of life.

As a Qigong practitioner, you should trace back its history to see how it was developed. Understanding the past makes it possible for you to avoid repeating the mistakes that other people have made. It also helps you to develop an appreciation for the art, which is necessary in pursuing your own study.

For these reasons, we will devote the rest of this chapter to defining Qi and Qigong and reviewing the history of Qigong and Taijiquan. We will also introduce the general concepts which are critical in understanding the why and how of your Qigong practice. In the second chapter, we will discuss the Yin and Yang of Taijiquan. This will give you an understanding of Taiji Qigong's place in Chinese Qigong. Finally, in the third chapter we will introduce several sets of Taiji Qigong exercises.

1.2 The Definition of Qi and Qigong

What is Qi? In order to understand Qigong, you must first understand what Qi is. Qi is the energy or natural force which fills the universe. There are three general types of Qi. The heavens (the sky or universe) have Heaven Qi (Tian Qi, 天氣), which is made up of the forces which the heavenly bodies exert on the earth, such as sunshine, moonlight, and the moon's effect on the tides. The Earth has Earth Qi (Di Qi, 地氣), which absorbs the Heaven Qi, and is influenced by it. Mankind has Human Qi (Ren Qi, 人氣), which is influenced by the other two. In ancient times, the Chinese believed that it was Heaven Qi which controlled the weather, climate, and natural disasters. When this Qi or energy field loses its balance, it strives to re-balance itself. Then the wind must blow, rain must fall, even tornadoes and hurricanes must happen in order for the Heaven Qi to reach a new energy balance. Heaven Qi also affects Human Qi, and divination and astrology are attempts to explain this.

Under Heaven Qi is the Earth Qi. It is influenced and controlled by the Heaven Qi. For example, too much rain will force a river to flood or change its path. Without rain, the plants will die. The Chinese believe that Earth Qi is made up of lines and patterns of energy, as well as the earth's magnetic field and the heat concealed underground. These energies must also balance, otherwise disasters such as earthquakes will occur. When the Qi of the earth is balanced, plants will grow and animals will prosper. Also, each individual person, animal, and plant has its own Qi field, which always seeks to be balanced. When any individual life loses its balance, it will sicken, die, and decompose.

You must understand that all natural things, including man, grow within, and are influenced by, the natural cycles of Heaven Qi and Earth Qi. Since you are part of this nature (Dao), you must understand Heaven Qi and Earth Qi. Then you will be able to adjust yourself, when necessary, to fit more smoothly into the natural cycle, and you will learn how to protect yourself from the negative influences in nature. This is the major target of Qigong practice.

From this you can see that in order to have a long and healthy life, the first rule is that you must live in harmony with the cycles of nature, and avoid and prevent negative influences. The Chinese have researched nature for thousands of years. Some of the information on the patterns and cycles of nature has been recorded in books, one of which is the *Yi Jing (Classic of Changes)*. This book gives the average person formulas to trace when the season will change, when it will snow, when a farmer should plow or harvest. You must remember that nature is always repeating itself. If you observe carefully, you will be able to see many of these routine patterns and cycles caused by the rebalancing of the Qi fields.

For thousands of years the Chinese have researched the interrelationships of all things in nature, especially with regard to human beings. From this experience they have created various Qigong exercises to help bring the body's Qi circulation into harmony with nature's cycles. This helps to avoid illnesses caused by weather or seasonal changes.

The Chinese also discovered that through Qigong they were able to strengthen their Qi circulation and slow down the degeneration of the body, gaining not only health but also a longer life. The realization that such things were possible greatly spurred new research.

What is Qigong? You can see from the preceding discussion that Qi is energy, and it is found in the heavens, in the earth, and in every living thing. All of these different types of energy interact with each other, and can transform into one another. In China, the word "Gong" (功) is often used instead of "Gongfu" (功夫), which means energy and time. Any study or training which requires a lot of energy and time to learn or to accomplish is called Gongfu. The term can be applied to any special skill or study as long as it requires time, energy, and patience. Therefore, the correct definition of Qigong is any training or study dealing with Qi which takes a long time and a lot of effort.

Qi exists in everything, from the largest to the smallest. Since the range of Qi is so vast, the Chinese have divided it into three categories, parallel to the Three Powers (San Cai, 三才) of Heaven, Earth, and Man. Generally speaking, Heaven Qi is the biggest and the most powerful. This Heaven Qi contains within it the Earth Qi, and within this Heaven and Earth Qi lives man, with his own Qi. You can see that Human Qi is part of Heaven Qi and Earth Qi. However, since the human beings who research Qi are mainly interested in Human Qi, the term Qigong is usually used to refer only to Qi training for people.

Qigong research should ideally include Heaven Qi, Earth Qi, and Human Qi. Understanding Heaven Qi is very difficult, however, and it was especially so in ancient times when the science was just developing. The major rules and principles relating to Heaven Qi can be found in such books as *The Five Elements* and *Ten Stems, Celestial Stems,* and the *Yi Jing* (易經).

Many people have become proficient in the study of Earth Qi. They are called Di Li Shi (Geomancy Teachers, 地理師) or Feng Shui Shi (Wind Water Teachers, 風水師). These experts use the accumulated body of geomantic knowledge and the *Yi Jing* to help people make important decisions such as where and how to build a house, or even where to locate a grave. This profession is still quite common in China.

The Chinese people believe that Human Qi is affected and controlled by Heaven Qi and Earth Qi, and that they in fact determine your destiny. Some people specialize in explaining these connections; they are called Suan Ming Shi (Calculate Life Teachers, 算命師), or fortune tellers.

Most Qigong research has focused on Human Qi. Since Qi is the source of life, if you understand how Qi functions and know how to affect it correctly, you should be able to live a long and healthy life. Many different aspects of Human Qi have been researched, including acupuncture, acupressure, massage, herbal treatment, meditation, and Qigong exercises. The use of acupuncture, acupressure, massage, and herbal treatment to adjust Human Qi flow has become the root of Chinese medical science. Meditation and moving Qigong exercises are widely used by the Chinese people to improve their health or even to cure certain illnesses. Meditation and Qigong exercises serve an additional role in that Daoists and Buddhists use them in their spiritual pursuit of enlightenment and Buddhahood.

You can see that the study of any of the aspects of Qi should be called Qigong. However, since the term is usually used today only in reference to the cultivation of Human Qi, we will use it only in this narrower sense to avoid confusion.

1.3 A Brief History of Qigong

The history of Chinese Qigong can be roughly divided into four periods. We know little about the first period, which is considered to have started when the *Yi Jing (Book of Changes)* was introduced sometime before 1122 B.C., and to have extended until the Han dynasty (206 B.C., 漢) when Buddhism and its meditation methods migrated from India. This infusion brought Qigong practice and meditation into the second period, the religious Qigong era. This period lasted until the Liang dynasty (502-557 A.D., 梁), when it was discovered that Qigong could be used for martial purposes. This was the beginning of the third period, that of martial Qigong. Many different martial Qigong styles were created based on the theories and principles of Buddhist and Daoist Qigong. This period lasted until the overthrow of the Qing dynasty (清) in 1912, when the new era started in which Chinese Qigong training is being mixed with Qigong practices from India, Japan, and many other countries.

Before the Han Dynasty (Before 206 B.C.). The *Yi Jing* (*Book of Changes*; 1122 B.C.) was probably the first Chinese book related to Qi. It introduced the concept of the three natural energies or powers (San Cai, 三才): Tian (Heaven, 天), Di (Earth, 地), and Ren (Man, 人). Studying the relationship of these three natural powers was the first step in the development of Qigong.

In 1766-1122 B.C. (the Shang Dynasty, 商), the Chinese capital was in today's An Yang in Henan province (河南安陽). An archaeological dig there at a late Shang dynasty burial ground called Yin Shiu discovered more than 160,000 pieces of turtle shell and animal bone which were covered with written characters. This writing, called *Jia Gu Wen* (Oracle-Bone Scripture, 甲骨文), was the earliest evidence of the Chinese use of the written word. Most of the information recorded was of a religious nature. There was no mention of acupuncture or other medical knowledge, even though it was recorded in the Nei Jing (內經) that during the reign of the Yellow Emperor (2697-2597 B.C., 黃帝) Bian Shi (Stone Probes, 砭石) were already being used to adjust people's Qi circulation.

During the Zhou Dynasty (1122-255 B.C., 周), Lao Zi (老子)(or Li Er, 李耳) mentioned certain breathing techniques in his classic *Dao De Jing* (*Classic on the Virtue of the Dao*, 道德經). He stressed that the way to obtain health was to "concentrate on Qi and achieve softness" (Zhuan Qi Zhi Rou).[1] Later, *Shi Ji* (*Historical Record*, 史紀) in the Spring and Autumn and Warring States Periods (722-222 B.C., 春秋戰國) also described more complete methods of breath training. About 300 B.C. the Daoist philosopher Zhuang Zi (莊子) described the relationship between health and breathing in his book *Nan Hua Jing* (南華經). It states: "The real person's (i.e., immortal's) breath reaches down to their heels. The normal person breathes in the throat."[2] This was not a figure of speech; it strongly suggests that a breathing method for Qi circulation was being used by some Daoists at that time.

During the Qin and Han dynasties (255 B.C.-221 A.D., 秦、漢) there are several medical references to Qigong in the literature, such as the *Nan Jing* (*Classic on Disorders*, 難經) by the famous doctor Bian Que (扁鵲), which describes using breathing to increase Qi circulation. *Jin Hui Yao Lue* (*Prescriptions from the Golden Chamber*, 金匱要略) by Zhang, Zhong-Jing (張仲景) discusses the use of breathing and acupuncture to maintain good Qi flow. *Zhou Yi Can Tonng Qi* (*A Comparative Study of the Zhou (dynasty) Book of Changes*, 周易參同契) by Wei, Bo-Yang (魏伯陽) explains the relationship of human beings to nature's forces and Qi. You can see that during this period almost all of the Qigong publications were written by scholars such as Lao Zi (老子) and Zhuang Zi (莊子), or medical doctors such as Bian Que (扁鵲) and Wei, Bo-Yang (魏伯陽).

From the Han Dynasty to the Beginning of the Liang Dynasty (206 B.C.-502 A.D.). Because many Han emperors were intelligent and wise, the Han Dynasty was a glorious and peaceful period. It was during the Eastern Han Dynasty (c. 58 A.D., 東漢) that Buddhism was imported to China from India. The Han Emperor became a sincere Buddhist, and Buddhism soon spread and became very popular. Many Buddhist meditation and Qigong practices, which had been used in India for thousands of years, were absorbed into the Chinese culture. The Buddhist temples taught many Qigong practices, especially the still meditation of Chan (禪)(or Ren, 忍), which marked a new era of Chinese Qigong. Much of the deeper Qigong theory and practices which had been developed in India were brought to China. Unfortunately, since the training was directed at attaining Buddhahood, the training practices and theory were recorded in the Buddhist bibles and kept secret. For hundreds of years the religious Qigong training was never taught to laymen. Only in this century has it been available to the general populace.

Not long after Buddhism came to China, a Daoist by the name of Zhang, Dao-Ling (張道陵) combined the traditional Daoist principles with Buddhism and created a religion called Dao Jiao (Dao religion, 道教). Many of the meditation methods were a combination of the principles and training methods of both sources.

Since Tibet had its own branch of Buddhism with its own training system and methods of attaining Buddhahood, Tibetan Buddhists were also invited to China to preach. In time, their practices were also absorbed.

It was in this period that the traditional Chinese Qigong practitioners finally had a chance to compare their arts with the religious Qigong practices imported mainly from India. While the scholarly and medical Qigong had been concerned with maintaining and improving health, the newly imported religious Qigong was concerned with far more. Contemporary documents and Qigong styles show clearly that the religious practitioners trained their Qi to a much deeper level, working with many internal functions of the body, and strove to have control of their bodies, minds, and spirits with the goal of escaping from the cycle of reincarnation.

While the Qigong practices and meditations were being passed down secretly within the monasteries, traditional scholars and physicians continued their Qigong research. During the Jin Dynasty (晉), in the 3rd century A.D., a famous physician named Hua Tuo (華陀) used acupuncture for anesthesia in surgery. The Daoist Jun Qian (君倩) used the movements of animals to create the Wu Qin Xi (Five Animal Sports, 五禽戲), which taught people how to increase their Qi circulation through specific movements. Also, in this period a physician named Ge Hong (葛洪) mentioned using the mind to lead and increase Qi in his book *Bao Pu Zi* (抱朴子). Sometime in the period of 420 to 581 A.D. Tao, Hong-Jing (陶弘景) compiled the *Yang Shen Yan Ming Lu* (*Records of Nourishing the Body and Extending Life*, 養身延命錄), which showed many Qigong techniques.

From the Liang Dynasty to the End of the Qing Dynasty (592-1912 A.D.). During the Liang Dynasty (502-557 A.D., 梁) the emperor invited a Buddhist monk named Da Mo (達磨), who was once an Indian prince, to preach Buddhism in China. When the emperor decided he did not like Da Mo's Buddhist theory, the monk withdrew to the Shaolin Temple (少林寺). When Da Mo arrived, he saw that the priests were weak and sickly, so he shut himself away to ponder the problem. He emerged after nine years of seclusion and wrote two classics: *Yi Jin Jing* (*Muscle/Tendon Changing Classic*, 易筋經) and *Xi Sui Jing* (*Marrow/Brain Washing Classic*, 洗髓經). The *Muscle/Tendon Changing Classic* taught the priests how to gain health and change their physical bodies from weak to strong. The *Marrow/Brain Washing Classic* taught the priests how to use Qi to clean the bone marrow and strengthen the blood and immune systems, as well as how to energize the brain and attain enlightenment. Because the *Marrow/Brain Washing Classic* was harder to understand and practice, the training methods were passed down secretly to only a very few disciples in each generation.

After the priests practiced the Muscle/Tendon Changing exercises, they found that not only did they improve their health, but they also greatly increased their strength. When this training was integrated into the martial arts forms, it increased the effectiveness of their techniques. In addition to this martial Qigong training, the Shaolin priests also created five animal styles of Gongfu which imitated the way different animals fight. The animals imitated were the tiger, leopard, dragon, snake, and crane.

Outside of the monastery, the development of Qigong continued during the Sui and Tang dynasties (581-907 A.D., 隋、唐). Chao, Yuan-Fang (巢元方) compiled the *Zhu Bing Yuan Hou Lun* (*Thesis on the Origins and Symptoms of Various Diseases*, 諸病源候論), which is a veritable encyclopedia of Qigong methods listing 260 different ways of increasing the Qi flow. The *Qian Jin Fang* (Thousand Gold Prescriptions, 千金方) by Sun, Si-Miao (孫思邈) described the method of leading Qi, and also described the use of the Six Sounds. The use of the Six Sounds to regulate Qi in the internal Organs had already been used by the Buddhists and Daoists for some time. Sun, Si-Miao also introduced a massage system called *Lao Zi's Forty-Nine Massage Techniques*. *Wai Tai Mi Yao* (*The Extra Important Secret*, 外台密要) by Wang Tao (王燾) discussed the use of breathing and herbal therapies for disorders of Qi circulation.

During the Song, Jin, and Yuan Dynasties (960-1368 A.D., 宋、金、元), *Yang Shen Jue* (*Life Nourishing Secrets*, 養身訣) by Zhang, An-Dao (張安道) discussed several Qigong practices. *Ru Men Shi Shi* (*The Confucian Point of View*, 儒門視事) by Zhang, Zi-He (張子和) describes the use of Qigong to cure external injuries such as cuts and sprains. *Lan Shi Mi Cang* (*Secret Library of the Orchid Room*, 蘭室密藏) by Li Guo (李杲) describes using Qigong and herbal remedies for internal disorders. *Ge Zhi Yu Lun* (*A Further Thesis of Complete Study*, 格致餘論) by Zhu, Dan-Xi (朱丹溪) provided a theoretical explanation for the use of Qigong in curing disease.

During the Song Dynasty (960-1279 A.D., 宋), Zhang, San-Feng (張三豐) is believed to have created Taijiquan. Taiji followed a different approach in its use of Qigong than did Shaolin. While Shaolin emphasized Wai Dan (External Elixir, 外丹) Qigong exercises, Taiji emphasized Nei Dan (Internal Elixir, 內丹) Qigong training.

In 1026 A.D. the famous brass man of acupuncture was designed and built by Dr. Wang, Wei-Yi (王唯一). Before this time, although there were many publications which discussed acupuncture theory, principles, and treatment techniques, there were many disagreements among them, and many points which were unclear. When Dr. Wang built his brass man, he also wrote a book called *Tong Ren Yu Xue Zhen Jiu Tu* (*Illustration of the Brass Man Acupuncture and Moxibustion*, 銅人俞穴針灸圖). He explained the relationship of the twelve organs and the twelve Qi channels, clarified many of the points of confusion, and, for the first time, systematically organized acupuncture theory and principles.

In 1034 A.D. Dr. Wang used acupuncture to cure the emperor Ren Zong (仁宗). With the support of the emperor, acupuncture flourished. In order to encourage acupuncture medical research, the emperor built a temple to Bian Que (扁鵲), who wrote the Nan Jing (難經), and worshiped him as the ancestor of acupuncture. Acupuncture technology developed so much that even the Jin race (金) in the North requested the brass man and other acupuncture technology as a condition for peace. Between 1102 to 1106 A.D. Dr. Wang dissected the bodies of prisoners and added more information to the Nan Jing. His work contributed greatly to the advancement of Qigong and Chinese medicine by giving a clear and systematic idea of the circulation of Qi in the human body.

Later, in the Southern Song Dynasty (1127-1279 A.D., 南宋), Marshal Yue Fei (岳飛) was credited with creating several internal Qigong exercises and martial arts. It is said that he created the Eight Pieces of Brocade (Ba Duan Jin, 八段錦) to improve the health of his soldiers. He is also known as the creator of the internal martial style Xingyiquan (形意拳). Eagle style martial artists also claim that Yue Fei was the creator of their style.

From then until the end of the Qing Dynasty (1912 A.D., 清), many other Qigong styles were founded. The well known ones include Hu Bu Gong (Tiger Step Gong, 虎步功), Shi Er Zhuang (Twelve Postures, 十二庄) and Jiao Hua Gong (Beggar Gong, 叫化功). Also in this period, many documents related to Qigong were published, such as *Bao Shen Mi Yao* (*The Secret Important Document of Body Protection*, 保身祕要) by Cao, Yuan-Bai (曹元白), which described moving and stationary Qigong practices; and *Yang Shen Fu Yu* (*Brief Introduction to Nourishing the Body*, 養身膚語) by Chen, Ji-Ru (陳繼儒), about the three treasures: Jing (Essence, 精), Qi (Internal Energy, 氣), and Shen (Spirit, 神). Also, *Yi Fang Ji Jie* (*The Total Introduction to Medical Prescriptions*, 醫方集介) by Wang, Fan-An (汪汎庵) reviewed and summarized the previously published materials; and *Nei Gong Tu Shuo* (*Illustrated Explanation of Internal Gong*, 內功圖說) by Wang, Zu-Yuan (王祖源) presented the *Twelve Pieces of Brocade* (Shi Er Duan Jin, 十二段錦) and explained the idea of combining both moving and stationary Qigong.

In the late Ming dynasty (around 1640 A.D., 明), a martial Qigong style, Huo Long Gong (Fire Dragon Gong, 火龍功) was created by the Tai Yang (太陽) martial stylists. The well known internal martial art style Baguazhang (Eight Trigrams Palm, 八卦掌) is believed to have been created by Dong Hai-Chuan (董海川) late in the Qing dynasty (1644-1912 A.D., 清). This style is now gaining in popularity throughout the world.

During the Qing dynasty, Tibetan meditation and martial techniques became widespread in China for the first time. This was due to the encouragement and interest of the Manchurian

Emperors in the royal palace, as well as others of high rank in society.

From the End of Qing Dynasty to the Present. Before 1912 A.D., Chinese society was still very conservative and old fashioned. Even though China had been expanding its contact with the outside world for the previous hundred years, the outside world had little influence beyond the coastal regions. With the overthrow of the Qing dynasty in 1912 and the rounding of the Chinese Republic, the nation started changing as never before. Since this time Qigong practice has entered a new era. Because of the ease of communication in the modern world, Western culture is having a great influence on the Orient. Many Chinese have opened their minds and changed their traditional ideas, especially in Taiwan and Hong Kong. Various Qigong styles are now being taught openly, and many formerly secret documents have been published. Modern methods of communication have opened up Qigong to a much wider audience than ever before, and people now have the chance to study and understand many different styles. In addition, people are now able to compare Chinese Qigong to similar arts from other countries such as India, Japan, Korea, and the Middle East.

In the near future Qigong could be considered the most exciting and challenging field of research. It is an ancient science just waiting to be investigated with the help of the new technologies now being developed at an almost explosive rate. Anything we can do to speed up this research will greatly help humanity to understand and improve itself.

1.4 Categories of Qigong

Generally speaking, all Qigong practices can be divided according to their training theory and methods into two general categories: Wai Dan (External Elixir) and Nei Dan (Internal Elixir). Understanding the differences between them will give you an overview of most Chinese Qigong practices.

■ **1.4.1 Wai Dan (External Elixir, 外丹)**

"Wai" means "external or outside," and "Dan" means "elixir." External here means the limbs, as opposed to the torso, which includes all of the vital organs. Elixir is a hypothetical, life-prolonging substance for which Chinese Daoists have been searching for millennia. They originally thought that the elixir was something physical which could be prepared from herbs or chemicals purified in a furnace. After thousands of years of study and experimentation, they found that the elixir is in the body. In other words, if you want to prolong your life, you must find the elixir in your body, and then learn to protect and nourish it.

In Wai Dan Qigong practice, you concentrate your attention on your limbs. As you exercise, the Qi builds up in your arms and legs. When the Qi potential in your limbs builds to a high enough level, the Qi will flow through the channels, clearing any obstructions and nourishing the organs. This is the main reason that a person who works out, or has a physical job, is generally healthier than someone who sits around all day.

■ 1.4.2 Nei Dan (Internal Elixir, 內丹)

"Nei" means "internal" and "Dan" means "elixir." Thus, Nei Dan means to build the elixir internally. Here, internally means in the body instead of in the limbs. Whereas in Wai Dan the Qi is built up in the limbs and then moved into the body, Nei Dan exercises build up Qi in the body and lead it out to the limbs.

Generally speaking, Nei Dan theory is deeper than Wai Dan theory, and it is more difficult to understand and practice. Traditionally, most of the Nei Dan Qigong practices have been passed down more secretly than those of the Wai Dan. This is especially true of the highest levels of Nei Dan, such as Marrow/Brain Washing, which were passed down to only a few trusted disciples.

We can also classify Qigong into four major categories according to the purpose or final goal of the training: 1. maintaining health; 2. curing sickness; 3. martial skill; and 4. enlightenment or Buddhahood. This is only a rough breakdown, however, since almost every style of Qigong serves more than one of the above purposes. For example, although martial Qigong focuses on increasing fighting effectiveness, it can also improve your health. The Daoist Qigong aims for longevity and enlightenment, but to reach this goal you need to be in good health and know how to cure sickness. Because of this multi-purpose aspect of the categories, it will be simpler to discuss their backgrounds rather than the goals of their training. Knowing the history and basic principles of each category will help you to understand their Qigong more clearly.

Scholar Qigong—for Maintaining Health. In China before the Han dynasty (206 B.C.-221 A.D., 漢), there were two major branches of scholarship. One of them was created by Confucius (551-479 B.C., 孔子) during the Spring and Autumn Period (Chun Qiu, 722-484 B.C., 春秋). The scholars who practice his philosophy are commonly called Confucians. Later, his philosophy was popularized and enlarged by Mencius (372-289 B.C., 孟子) in the Warring States Period (Zhan Guo, 403-222 B.C., 戰國). The people who practice this are called Ru Jia (Confucianists, 儒家). The key words to their basic philosophy are Loyalty (Zhong, 忠), Filial Piety (Xiao, 孝), Humanity (Ren, 仁), Kindness (Ai, 愛), Trust (Xin, 信), Justice (Yi, 義), Harmony (He, 和), and Peace (Ping, 平). Humanity and human feelings are the main subjects of study. Ru Jia philosophy has become the center of much Chinese culture.

The second major school of scholarship was called Dao Jia (Daoism, 道家) and was created by Lao Zi (老子) in the 6th century B.C. Lao Zi is considered to be the author of a book called the *Dao De Jing (Classic on the Virtue of the Dao*, 道德經) which described human morality. Later, in the Warring States Period, his follower Zhuang Zhou (莊周) wrote a book called *Zhuang Zi* (莊子), which led to the forming of another strong branch of Daoism. Before the Han dynasty, Daoism was considered a branch of scholarship. However, in the Han dynasty traditional Daoism was combined with the Buddhism imported from India, and it began gradually to be treated as a religion (Dao Jiao, 道教). Therefore, the Daoism before the Han dynasty should be considered scholarly Daoism rather than religious.

With regard to their contribution to Qigong, both schools of scholarship emphasized maintaining health and preventing disease. They believed that many illnesses are caused by mental and emotional excesses. When a person's mind is not calm, balanced, and peaceful, the organs will not function normally. For example, depression can cause stomach ulcers and indigestion. Anger will cause the liver to malfunction. Sadness will cause stagnation and tightness in the lungs, and fear can disturb the normal functioning of the kidneys and bladder. They realized that if you want to avoid illness, you must learn to balance and relax your thoughts and emotions. This is called "regulating the mind."

Therefore, the scholars emphasized gaining a peaceful mind through meditation. In their still meditation, the main training is eliminating thoughts so that the mind is clear and calm. When you become calm, the flow of thoughts and emotions slows down, and you feel mentally and emotionally neutral. This kind of meditation can be thought of as practicing emotional self-control. When you are in this "no thought" state, you become very relaxed, and can even relax deep down into your internal organs. When your body is this relaxed, your Qi will naturally flow smoothly and strongly. This kind of still meditation was very common in ancient Chinese scholarly society.

In order to reach the goal of a calm and peaceful mind, their training focused on regulating the mind, body, and breath. They believed that as long as these three things were regulated, the Qi flow would be smooth and sickness would not occur. This is why the Qi training of the scholars is called "Xiu Qi" (修氣), which means "cultivating Qi." Xiu in Chinese means to regulate, to cultivate, or to repair. It means to maintain in good condition. This is very different from the religious Daoist Qi training after the Han dynasty which was called "Lian Qi" (練氣), which is translated "train Qi." Lian means to drill or to practice to make stronger.

Many of the Qigong documents written by the Confucians and Daoists were limited to the maintenance of health. The scholar's attitude in Qigong was to follow his natural destiny and maintain his health. This philosophy is quite different from that of the religious Daoists after the Han dynasty, who denied that one's destiny could not be changed. They believed that it is possible to train your Qi to make it stronger, and to extend your life. It is said in scholarly society: "Ren Shen Qi Shi Gu Lai Xi,"[3] which means "in human life seventy is rare." You should understand that few of the common people in ancient times lived past seventy because of the lack of good food and modern medical technology. It is also said: "An Tian Le Ming,"[4] which means "peace with heaven and delight in your destiny"; and "Xiu Shen Shi Ming,"[5] which means "cultivate the body and await destiny." Compare this with the philosophy of the later Daoists, who said: "Yi Bai Er Shi Wei Zhi Yao,"[6] which means "one hundred and twenty means dying young." They believed and have proven that human life can be lengthened and destiny can be resisted and overcome.

Confucianism and Daoism were the two major schools of scholarship in China, but there were many other schools which were also more or less involved in Qigong exercises. We will not discuss them here because there is only a limited number of Qigong documents from these schools.

Medical Qigong—for Healing. In ancient Chinese society, most emperors respected the scholars and were affected by their philosophy. Doctors were not highly regarded because they made their diagnosis by touching the patient's body, which was considered characteristic of the lower classes in society. Despite this, the doctors developed a profound and successful medical science. However, they continued to work hard and study, and quietly passed down the results of their research to following generations.

Of all the groups studying Qigong in China, the doctors have been at it the longest. Since the discovery of Qi circulation in the human body about four thousand years ago, Chinese doctors have devoted a major portion of their efforts to studying the behavior of Qi. Their efforts resulted in acupuncture, acupressure or cavity press massage, and herbal treatment.

In addition, many Chinese doctors used their medical knowledge to create different sets of Qigong exercises either for maintaining health or for curing specific illnesses. Chinese medical doctors believed that doing only sitting or still meditation to regulate the body, mind, and breathing—as the scholars did—was not enough to cure sickness. They believed that in order to increase the Qi circulation, you must move. Although a calm and peaceful mind was important for health, exercising the body was more important. They learned through their medical practice that people who exercised properly got sick less often, and their bodies degenerated less quickly than was the case with people who just sat around. They also realized that specific body movements could increase the Qi circulation in specific organs. They reasoned from this that these exercises could also be used to treat specific illnesses and to restore the normal functioning of these organs.

Some of these movements are similar to the way in which certain animals move. It is clear that in order for an animal to survive in the wild, it must have an instinct for how to protect its body. Part of this instinct is concerned with how to build up its Qi, and how to keep its Qi from being lost. We humans have lost many of these instincts over the years that we have been separating ourselves from nature.

Many doctors developed Qigong exercises which were modeled after animal movements to maintain health and cure sickness. A typical, well known set of such exercises is "Wu Qin Xi" (Five Animal Sports, 五禽戲) created by Dr. Jun Qian (君倩). Another famous set based on similar principles is called "Ba Duan Jin" (The Eight Pieces of Brocade, 八段錦). It was created by Marshal Yue Fei (岳飛) who, interestingly enough, was a soldier rather than a doctor.

In addition, using their medical knowledge of Qi circulation, Chinese doctors researched until they found which movements could help cure particular illnesses and health problems. Not surprisingly, many of these movements were not unlike the ones used to maintain health, since many illnesses are caused by unbalanced Qi. When an imbalance continues for a long period of time, the organs will be affected, and may be physically damaged. It is just like running a machine without supplying the proper electrical current—over time, the machine will be damaged. Chinese doctors believe that before physical damage to an organ shows up in a patient's body, there is first an abnormality in the Qi balance and circulation. Abnormal Qi circulation is the very beginning of illness and physical organ damage. When Qi is too positive (Yang) or too negative (Yin) in a specific organ's Qi channel, your physical organ is beginning to suffer damage. If you do not correct the Qi circulation, that organ will malfunction or degenerate. The best way to heal someone is to adjust and balance the Qi even before there is any physical problem. Therefore, correcting or increasing the normal Qi circulation is the major goal of acupuncture or acupressure treatments. Herbs and special diets are also considered important treatments in regulating the Qi in the body

As long as the illness is limited to the level of Qi stagnation and there is no physical organ damage, the Qigong exercises used for maintaining health can be used to readjust the Qi circulation and treat the problem. However, if the sickness is already so serious that the physical organs have started to fail, then the situation has become critical and a specific treatment is necessary. The treatment can be acupuncture, herbs, or even an operation, as well as specific Qigong exercises designed to speed up the healing or even to cure the sickness. For example, ulcers and asthma can often be cured or helped by some simple exercises. Recently in both mainland China and Taiwan, certain Qigong exercises have been shown to be effective in treating certain kinds of cancer.[7]

After years of observing nature and themselves, some Qigong practitioners went even deeper. They realized that the body's Qi circulation changes with the seasons, and that it is a good idea to help the body out during these periodic adjustments. They noticed also that in each season different organs have characteristic problems. For example, in the beginning of autumn the lungs have to adapt to the colder air that you are breathing. While this adjustment is occurring, the lungs are susceptible to disturbance, so your lungs may feel uncomfortable and you may catch colds easily. Your digestive system is also affected during seasonal changes. Your appetite may increase, or you may have diarrhea. When the temperature goes down, your kidneys and bladder will start to give you trouble. For example, because the kidneys are stressed, you may feel pain in the back. Focusing on these seasonal Qi disorders, the meditators created a set of movements which can be used to speed up the body's adjustment. These Qigong exercises will be introduced in a later volume.

In addition to Marshal Yue Fei, many people who were not doctors also created sets of medical Qigong. These sets were probably originally created to maintain health, and later were also used for curing sickness.

Martial Qigong—for Fighting. Chinese martial Qigong was probably not developed until Da Mo (達磨) wrote the *Muscle/Tendon Changing Classic* in the Shaolin Temple during the Liang dynasty (502-557 A.D., 梁). When Shaolin monks trained Da Mo's Muscle/Tendon Changing Qigong, they found that they could not only improve their health but also greatly increase the power of their martial techniques. Since then, many martial styles have developed Qigong sets to increase their effectiveness. In addition, many martial styles have been created based on Qigong theory. Martial artists have played a major role in Chinese Qigong society.

When Qigong theory was first applied to the martial arts, it was used to increase the power and efficiency of the muscles. The theory is very simple—the mind (Yi, 意) is used to lead Qi to the muscles to energize them so that they function more efficiently. The average person generally uses his muscles at under forty percent maximum efficiency. If one can train his concentration and use his strong Yi (the mind generated from clear thinking) to lead Qi to the muscles effectively, he will be able to energize the muscles to a higher level and, therefore, increase his fighting effectiveness.

As acupuncture theory became better understood, fighting techniques were able to reach even more advanced levels. Martial artists learned to attack specific areas, such as vital acupuncture cavities, to disturb the enemy's Qi flow and create imbalances which caused injury or even death. In order to do this, it is necessary to understand the route and timing of the Qi circulation in the human body. A practitioner must train to strike the cavities accurately and to the correct depth. These cavity strike techniques are called "Dian Xue" (Pointing Cavities, 點穴) or "Dim Mak" (Cantonese) or "Dian Mai" (Pointing Vessels, 點脈).

Most martial Qigong practices help to improve the practitioner's health. However, there are other martial Qigong practices which, although they build up some special skill which is useful for fighting, also damage the practitioner's health. An example of this is Iron Sand Palm (Tie Sha Zhang, 鐵砂掌). Although this training can build up amazing destructive power, it can also harm your hands and affect the Qi circulation in the hands and the internal organs.

Since the 6th century, many martial styles have been created which were based on Qigong theory. They can be roughly divided into external and internal styles.

The external styles emphasize building Qi in the limbs to coordinate with the physical martial techniques. They follow the theory of Wai Dan (external elixir, 外丹) Qigong, which usually generates Qi in the limbs through special exercises. The concentrated mind is used during the exercises to energize the Qi. This increases muscular strength significantly, and therefore increases the effectiveness of the martial techniques. Qigong can also be used to train the body to resist punches and kicks. In this training, Qi is led to energize the skin and the muscles, enabling them to resist a blow without injury. This training is commonly called "Iron Shirt" (Tie Bu Shan, 鐵布衫) or "Golden Bell Cover" (Jin Zhong Zhao, 金鐘罩). The martial styles which use Wai Dan Qigong training are normally called external styles (Wai Gong, 外功) or hard styles (Ying Gong, 硬功). Shaolin Gongfu is a typical example of a style which uses Wai Dan martial Qigong.

Although Wai Dan Qigong can help the martial artist increase his power, there is a disadvantage. Because Wai Dan Qigong emphasizes training the external muscles, it can cause over-development. This can cause a problem called "energy dispersion" (San Gong, 散功) when the practitioner gets older. In order to remedy this, when an external martial artist reaches a high level of external Qigong training he will start training internal Qigong, which specializes in curing the energy dispersion problem. That is why it is said "Shaolin Gongfu from external to internal."

Internal Martial Qigong is based on the theory of Nei Dan (internal elixir, 內丹). In this method, Qi is generated in the body instead of the limbs, and this Qi is then led to the limbs to increase power. In order to lead Qi to the limbs, the techniques must be soft and muscle usage must be kept to a minimum. The training and theory of Nei Dan martial Qigong is much more difficult than those of Wai Dan martial Qigong. Interested readers should refer to the author's book: *Tai Chi Theory and Martial Power*, available from YMAA Publication Center.

Several internal martial styles were created in the Wudang (武當) and Emei (峨嵋) Mountains. Popular styles are Taijiquan (太極拳), Baguazhang (八卦掌), Liu He Ba Fa (六合八法), and Xingyiquan (形意拳). However, you should understand that even the internal martial styles, which are commonly called soft styles, must on some occasions use muscular strength while fighting. Therefore, once an internal martial artist has achieved a degree of competence in internal Qigong, he or she should also learn how to use harder, more external techniques. That is why it is said: "the internal styles are from soft to hard."

In the last fifty years, some of the Taiji Qigong or Taijiquan practitioners have developed training which is mainly for health, and is called "Wuji Qigong" (無極氣功), which means "no extremities Qigong." Wuji is the state of neutrality which precedes Taiji, which is the state of relative opposites. When there are thoughts and feelings in your mind, there is Yin and Yang, but if you can still your mind you can return to the emptiness of Wuji. When you achieve this state your mind is centered and clear and your body relaxed, and your Qi is able to flow naturally and smoothly and reach the proper balance by itself. Wuji Qigong has become very popular in many parts of China, especially Shanghai and Canton.

You can see that, although Qigong is widely studied in Chinese martial society, the main focus of training was originally on increasing fighting ability rather than health. Good health was considered a by-product of the training. It was not until this century that the health aspect of martial Qigong started receiving greater attention. This is especially true in the internal martial arts. Please refer to the author's in-depth martial Qigong book: *The Essence of Shaolin White Crane*.

Religious Qigong—for Enlightenment or Buddhahood. Religious Qigong, though not as popular as other categories in China, is recognized as having achieved the highest accomplishments of all the Qigong categories. It used to be kept secret, and it is only in this century that it has been revealed to laymen.

In China, religious Qigong includes mainly Daoist and Buddhist Qigong. The main purpose of their training is striving for enlightenment, or what the Buddhists refer to as Buddhahood. They are looking for a way to lift themselves above normal human suffering, and to escape from the cycle of continual reincarnation. They believe that all human suffering is caused by the seven emotions and six desires. If you are still bound to these emotions and desires, you will reincarnate after your death. To avoid reincarnation, you must train your spirit to reach a very high stage where it is strong enough to be independent after your death. This spirit will enter the heavenly kingdom and gain eternal peace. This training is hard to do in the everyday world, so practitioners frequently flee society and move into the solitude of the mountains, where they can concentrate all of their energies on self-cultivation.

Religious Qigong practitioners train to strengthen their internal Qi to nourish their spirit (Shen) until this spirit is able to survive the death of the physical body. Marrow/Brain Washing Qigong training is necessary to reach this stage. It enables them to lead Qi to the forehead, where the spirit resides, and raise the brain to a higher energy state. This training used to be restricted to only a few priests who had reached an advanced level. Tibetan Buddhists were also involved heavily in this training. Over the last two thousand years the Tibetan Buddhists, the Chinese Buddhists, and the Daoist have followed the same principles to become the three major religious schools of Qigong training.

This religious striving toward enlightenment or Buddhahood is recognized as the highest and most difficult level of Qigong. Many Qigong practitioners reject the rigors of this religious striving, and practice Marrow/Brain Washing Qigong solely for the purpose of longevity. It was these people who eventually revealed the secrets of Marrow/Brain Washing to the outside world. If you are interested in knowing more about this training, you may refer to: *Muscle/Tendon Changing* and *Marrow/Brain Washing Chi Kung* by Dr. Yang.

1.5 A Brief History of Taijiquan

Qi theory and Qigong were not applied to the Chinese martial arts until the late Liang dynasty (502-557 A.D., 梁). This Qigong can be classified as either "external" or "internal." The external styles energize the muscles in the limbs with Qi so that they can manifest their maximum strength. Naturally, such training also develops the muscles. The internal styles believe that, in order for the physical body to manifest its maximum power, the most important thing was learning how to circulate and build up the Qi. Only then could the physical body be energized effectively. Their training therefore focused on circulating and building up the Qi internally. To do this, the body must remain relaxed and, to a degree, soft. Taijiquan belongs to this internal category.

It is said that Taijiquan was created by Zhang, San-Feng (張三豐) in the Song Hui Zong era (c. 1101 A.D., 宋徽宗). It is also said that techniques and forms with the same basic principles were already in existence during the Liang dynasty (502-557 A.D., 梁), and were being taught by Han, Gong-Yue (韓拱月), Cheng, Ling-Xi (程靈洗), and Cheng Bi (程珌). Later, in the Tang dynasty (618-907 A.D., 唐), it was found that Xu, Xuan-Ping (許宣平), Li, Dao-Zi (李道子), and Yin, Li-Hen (殷利亨) were teaching similar martial techniques. They were called Thirty-Seven Postures (San Shi Qi Shi, 三十七勢), Post-Heaven Techniques (Hou Tian

Fa, 後天法), or Small Nine Heaven (Xiao Jiu Tian, 小九天), which had seventeen postures. The accuracy of these accounts is questionable, so it is not really known when and by whom Taijiquan was created. Because there is more formal history recorded about Zhang, San-Feng, he has received most of the credit.

According to the historical record Nan Lei Ji Wang Zheng Nan Mu Zhi Ming: "Zhang, San-Feng, in the Song dynasty, was a Wudang Daoist. Hui Zong (a Song Emperor) summoned him, but the road was blocked and he couldn't come. At night, (Hui Zong) dreamed Emperor Yuan (the first Jin emperor) taught him martial techniques. At dawn, he killed a hundred enemies by himself."[8] Also, recorded in the Ming history Ming Shi Fang Ji Zhuan: "Zhang, San-Feng, from Liao Dong Yi county. Named Quan-Yi. Also named Jun-Bao. San-Feng was his nickname. Because he did not keep himself neat and clean, also called Zhang, La-Ta (Sloppy Zhang). He was tall and big, shaped like a turtle, and had a crane's back. Large ears and round eyes. Beard long like a spear tassel. Wears only a priest's robe winter or summer. Will eat a bushel of food, or won't eat for several days or a few months. Can travel a thousand miles. Likes to have fun with people. Behaves as if nobody is around. Used to travel to Wudang with his disciples. Built a simple cottage and lived inside. In the 24th year of Hong Wu (around 1939), Ming Tai Zu (the first Ming emperor) heard of his name, and sent a messenger to look for him but he couldn't be found."[9]

It was also recorded in the Ming dynasty in Ming Lang Ying Qi Xiu Lei Gao: "Zhang the Immortal, named Jun-Bao, also named Quan-Yi, nicknamed Xuan-Xuan, also called Zhang, La-Ta. In the third year of Tian Shun (1460 A.D.) he visited Emperor Ming Ying Zong. A picture was drawn. The beard and mustache were straight, the back of the head had a tuft. Purple face and big stomach, with a bamboo hat in his hand. On the top of the picture was an inscription from the emperor honoring Zhang as 'Tong Wei Xian Hua Zhen Ren' (a genuine Daoist who finely discriminates and clearly understands much" (Figure 1-1).[10] The record is suspect, because if it were true, Zhang, San-Feng would have been at least 500 years old at that time. Other records state that Zhang, San-Feng's techniques were learned from the Daoist Feng, Yi-Yuan (馮一元). Another story tells that Zhang, San-Feng was an ancient hermit meditator. He saw a magpie fighting a snake, had a sudden understanding, and created Taijiquan.

After Zhang, San-Feng, there were Wang Zong (王宗) in Shaanxi province (陝西), Chen, Tong-Zhou (陳同州) in Wen County (溫州), Zhang, Song-Xi (張松溪) in Hai Yan (海鹽), Ye, Ji-Mei (葉繼美) in Si Ming (四明), Wang, Zong-Yue (王宗岳) in Shan You (山右), and Jiang Fa (蔣發) in Hebei (河北). The Taiji techniques were passed down and divided into two major styles, southern and northern. Later, Jiang Fa passed his art to the Chen family at Chen Jia Gou (Chen Village, 陳家溝) in Huai Qing County (懷慶府), Henan (河南). Taiji was then passed down for fourteen generations and divided into the Old and the New Styles. The Old style was carried on by Chen, Chang-Xing (陳長興) and the New Style was created by Chen, You-Ben (陳有本).

The Old Style successor Chen, Chang-Xing then passed the art down to his son, Geng-Yun (耕雲), and his Chen relatives, Chen, Huai-Yuan (陳懷遠) and Chen, Hua-Mei

(陳華梅). He also passed his Taiji outside of his family to Yang, Lu-Shan (楊露禪) and Li, Bo-Kui (李伯魁), both of Hebei province (河北). This Old Style is called Thirteen Postures Old Form (Shi San Shi Lao Jia, 十三勢老架). Later, Yang, Lu-Shan passed it down to his two sons, Yang, Ban-Hou (楊班侯) and Yang, Jian-Hou (楊健侯). Then, Jian-Hou passed the art to his two sons, Yang, Shao-Hou (楊少侯) and Yang, Cheng-Fu (楊澄甫). This branch of Taijiquan is popularly called Yang Style (楊氏). Also, Wu, Quan-You (吳全佑) learned from Yang, Ban-Hou and started a well known Wu Style (吳氏).

Also, Chen, You-Ben passed his New Style to Chen, Qing-Ping (陳清萍) who created Zhao Bao Style Taijiquan (趙堡). Wuu, Yu-Rang (武禹讓) learned the Old Style from Yang, Lu-Shan and New Style from Chen, Qing-Ping, and created Wuu Style Taijiquan (武氏). Li, Yi-Yu (李亦畬) learned the Wuu Style and created Li Style Taijiquan (李氏). He, Wei-Zhen (郝爲楨) obtained his art from Li style and created He Style Taijiquan (郝氏). Sun, Lu-Tang (孫祿堂) learned from He Style and created Sun Style (孫氏).

1.6 Qigong Theory

Many people think that Qigong is a difficult subject to comprehend. In some ways, this is true. However, you must understand one thing: regardless of how difficult the Qigong theory and practice of a particular style are, the basic theory and principles are very simple and remain the same for all of the Qigong styles. The basic theory and principles are the roots of the entire Qigong practice. If you understand these roots, you will be able to grasp the key to the practice and grow. All of the Qigong styles originated from these roots, but each one has blossomed differently.

In this section we will discuss these basic theories and principles. With this knowledge as a foundation, you will be able to understand not only what you should be doing, but also why you are doing it. Naturally, it is impossible to discuss all of the basic Qigong ideas in such a short section. However, it will offer beginners the key to open the gate into the spacious, four thousand year old garden of Chinese Qigong. If you wish to know more about the theory of Qigong, please refer to: *The Root of Chinese Qigong* by Dr. Yang.

Qi and Man. In order to use Qigong to maintain and improve your health, you must know that there is Qi in your body, and you must understand how it circulates and what you can do to insure that the circulation is smooth and strong.

You know from previous discussions that Qi is energy. It is a requirement for life. The Qi in your body cannot be seen, but it can be felt. This Qi can make your body feel too positive (too Yang) or too negative (too Yin).

Imagine that your physical body is a machine, and your Qi is the current that makes it run. Without the current the machine is dead and unable to function. For example, when you pinch yourself, you feel pain. Have you ever thought "how do I feel pain?" You might answer that it is because you have a nervous system in your body which perceives the pinch and sends a signal to the brain. However, there is more to it than that. The nervous system is material, and if it didn't have energy circulating in it, it wouldn't function. Qi is the energy which makes the nervous system and the other parts of your body work. When you pinch your skin, that area is stimulated and the Qi field is disturbed. Your brain is designed to sense this and other disturbances, and to interpret the cause.

According to Chinese Qigong and medicine, the Qi in your body is divided into two categories: Managing Qi (Ying Qi, 營氣)(which is often called Nutritive Qi) and Guardian Qi (Wei Qi, 衛氣). The Managing Qi is the energy which is sent to the organs so that they can function. The Guardian Qi is the energy which is sent to the surface of the body to form a shield to protect you from negative outside influences such as cold. In order to keep yourself healthy, you must learn how to manage these two Qi efficiently so they can serve you well.

Qi is classified as Yin because it can only be felt, while the physical body is classified as Yang because it can be seen. Yin is the root and source of the life which animates the Yang body (physical body) and manifests power or strength externally. Therefore, when the Qi is strong, the physical body can function properly and be healthy, and it can manifest a lot of power or strength.

In order to have a strong and healthy body, you must learn how to keep the Qi circulating in your body smoothly, and you must also learn how to build up an abundant store of Qi. In order to reach these two goals, you must first understand the Qi circulatory and storage system in your body.

Chinese doctors discovered long ago that the human body has twelve major channels and eight vessels through which the Qi circulates. The twelve channels are like rivers which distribute Qi throughout the body, and also connect the extremities (fingers and toes) to the internal organs. I would like to point out here that the "internal organs" of Chinese medicine do not necessarily correspond to the physical organs as understood in the West, but rather to a set of clinical functions similar to each other, and related to the organ system. The eight vessels, which are often referred to as the extraordinary vessels, function like reservoirs and regulate the distribution and circulation of Qi in your body.

When the Qi in the eight reservoirs is full and strong, the Qi in the rivers is strong and will be regulated efficiently. When there is stagnation in any of these twelve channels or rivers, the Qi which flows to the body's extremities and to the internal organs will be abnormal, and illness may develop. You should understand that every channel has its particular Qi flow strength, and every channel is different. All of these different levels of Qi strength are affected by your mind, the weather, the time of day, the food you have eaten, and even your mood. For example, when the weather is dry the Qi in the lungs will tend to be more positive than when it is moist. When you are angry, the Qi flow in your liver channel will be abnormal. The Qi strength in the different channels varies throughout the day in a regular cycle, and at any particular time one channel is strongest. For example, between 11:00 AM and 1:00 PM the Qi flow in the heart channel is the strongest. Furthermore, the Qi level of the same organ can be different from one person to another.

Whenever the Qi flow in the twelve rivers or channels is not normal, the eight reservoirs will regulate the Qi flow and bring it back to normal. For example, when you experience a sudden shock, the Qi flow in the bladder immediately becomes deficient. Normally the reservoir will immediately regulate the Qi in this channel so that you recover from the shock. However, if the reservoir Qi is also deficient, or if the effect of the shock is too great and there is not enough time to regulate the Qi, the bladder will suddenly contract, causing unavoidable urination.

When a person is sick because of an injury, his Qi level tends to be either too positive (excessive, Yang) or too negative (deficient, Yin). A Chinese physician would either use a prescription of herbs to adjust the Qi, or else he would insert acupuncture needles at various spots on the channels to inhibit the flow in some channels and stimulate the flow in others, so that balance can be restored. However, there is another alternative, and that is to use certain physical and mental exercises to adjust the Qi. In other words, to use Qigong.

In the last twenty years, Western medicine has gradually begun to accept the existence of Qi and its circulation in the human body. Several studies indicate that what the Chinese call "Qi" is the bioelectric circulation in the body. It is now generally accepted by Western medicine that imbalance of the bioelectric current is a cause of many illnesses. Modern science is now learning many things which will help us to better understand Qigong, and will also increase Western medicine's willingness to accept the validity of Qigong.

If Qi is the bioelectricity circulating in the human body, in order to maintain the circulation of Qi or bioelectricity there must be an EMF (electromotive force) generating an electric potential difference. It is like an electric circuit, which must be hooked up to a battery or other source of EMF before there can be a current.

There are two main purposes in Qigong training: first, to maintain the smooth circulation of Qi (bioelectricity), and second, to fill up the Qi vessels (Qi reservoirs) with Qi. In order to have smooth circulation of Qi we must regulate the electric potential difference which controls the Qi flow, and also remove all sources of resistance in the path of the circulation. In order to fill up the Qi vessels, we need to know how to increase the charge in our "battery."

At this point you may ask, "If we keep increasing the EMF of the battery (Qi reservoirs), won't the excess Qi flow overheat the circuit (make it too Yang)?" The answer is yes, this can happen. However, your body is different from a regular electric circuit in that it is alive and can change. When the Qi flow becomes stronger, your body will react and build itself up so that it can accept this new Qi flow. Qigong should be trained slowly and carefully so that, as you build up the Qi stored in your channels, your body has time to readjust itself. All of this also makes your body stronger and healthier.

You can see that the key to Qigong practice is, in addition to removing resistance from the Qi channels, maintaining or increasing the Qi level (EMF) in the Qi reservoirs (battery or capacitor). What are the energy sources in our daily life which supply energy to our body, or, expressed differently, what are the sources by which the EMF can be increased in the body's bioelectric circuit, which would increase the flow of bioelectricity? There are four major sources:

1. **Natural Energy.** Since your body is of electrically conductive material, its electromagnetic field is always affected by the sun, the moon, clouds, the earth's magnetic field, and by the other energy around you. The major influences are the sun's radiation, the moon's gravity, and the earth's magnetic field. These affect your Qi circulation significantly, and are therefore responsible for the pattern of your Qi circulation since you were formed. We are now also being greatly affected by the energy generated by modern technology, such as the electromagnetic waves generated by radios, TVs, microwave ovens, computer monitors, high tension power lines, electrical wiring, and many other things.

2. **Food and Air.** In order to maintain life, we take in food and air essence through the mouth and nose. These essences are then converted into Qi through biochemical reaction in the chest and digestive system (called Triple Burners in Chinese medicine). When the Qi is converted from the essence, an EMF is generated which circulates the Qi throughout the body. A major part of Qigong is devoted to getting the proper kinds of food and fresh air.

3. **Thinking.** The human mind is the most important and efficient source of bioelectric EMF. Any time you move to do something you must first generate an idea (Yi). This idea generates the EMF and leads the Qi to energize the appropriate muscles to carry out the desired motion. The more you can concentrate, the stronger the EMF you can generate, and the stronger the flow of Qi you can lead. Naturally, the stronger the flow of Qi you lead to the muscles, the more they will be energized. Because of this, the mind is considered the most important factor in Qigong training.

4. **Exercise.** Exercise converts the food Essence (fat) stored in your body into Qi, and therefore builds up the EMF. Many Qigong styles have been created which utilize movement for this purpose.

In Taiji Qigong, the mind and the movements are the two major sources of EMF, though the other two sources are also involved. For example, when you practice in the early morning you can absorb energy from the sun. When you meditate facing the south in the evening you align yourself with the earth's magnetic field. It is also advisable to eliminate greasy and other undesirable foods from your diet, and, if possible, to practice in the mountains where the air is fresh and clear.

1.7 General Concepts of Qigong Training

Before you start your Qigong training, you must first understand the three treasures of life—Jing (Essence, 精), Qi (Internal Energy, 氣), and Shen (Spirit, 神)—as well as their interrelationship. If you lack this understanding, you are missing the root of Qigong training, as well as the basic idea of Qigong theory. The main goals of Qigong training are to learn how to retain your Jing, strengthen and smoothen your Qi flow, and enlighten your Shen. To reach these goals you must learn how to regulate the body (Tiao Shen, 調身), regulate the breathing (Tiao Xi, 調息), regulate the mind (Tiao Xin, 調心), regulate the Qi (Tiao Qi, 調氣), and regulate the Shen (Tiao Shen, 調神).

Regulating the body includes understanding how to find and build the root of the body, as well as the root of the individual forms you are practicing. To build a firm root, you must know how to keep your center, how to balance your body, and most important of all, how to relax so that the Qi can flow.

Regulating the mind involves learning how to keep your mind calm, peaceful, and centered, so that you can judge situations objectively and lead Qi to the desired places. The mind is the main key to success in Qigong practice.

To regulate your breathing, you must learn how to breathe so that your breathing and your mind mutually correspond and cooperate. When you breathe this way, your mind will be able to attain peace more quickly, and therefore concentrate more easily on leading the Qi.

Regulating the Qi is one of the ultimate goals of Qigong practice. In order to regulate your Qi effectively you must first have regulated your body, mind, and breathing. Only then will your mind be clear enough to sense how the Qi is distributed in your body, and understand how to adjust it.

For Buddhist priests, who seek the enlightenment of the Buddha, regulating the Shen is the final goal of Qigong. This enables them to maintain a neutral, objective perspective of life, and this perspective is the eternal life of the Buddha. The average Qigong practitioner has lower goals. He raises his Shen in order to increase his concentration and enhance his vitality. This makes it possible for him to lead Qi effectively to his entire body so that it carries out the managing and guarding duties. This maintains his health and slows down the aging process.

If you understand these few things you will be able to quickly enter into the field of Qigong. Without all of these important elements, your training will be ineffective and your time will be wasted.

■ 1.7.1 THREE TREASURES—JING, QI, AND SHEN

Before you start any Qigong training you must first understand the three treasures (San Bao, 三寶): Jing (Essence, 精), Qi (Internal Energy, 氣), and Shen (Spirit, 神). They are also called the three origins or the three roots (San Yuan, 三元), because they are considered the origins and roots of your life. Jing means Essence, the most original and refined part. Jing is the original source and most basic part of every living thing, and determines its nature and characteristics. It is the root of life. Sperm is called Jing Zi (精子), which means "Essence of the Son," because it contains the Jing of the father which is passed on to his son (or daughter) and becomes the son's Jing.

Qi is the internal energy of your body. It is like the electricity which passes through a machine to keep it running. Qi comes either from the conversion of the Jing which you have received from your parents, or from the food you eat and the air you breathe.

Shen is the center of your mind and being. It is what makes you human, because animals do not have a Shen. The Shen in your body must be nourished by your Qi or energy. When your Qi is full, your Shen will be enlivened.

Chinese meditators and Qigong practitioners believe that the body contains two general types of Qi. The first type is called Pre-birth Qi (Xian Tian Qi, 先天氣), and it comes from converted Original Jing (Yuan Jing, 元精), which you get from your parents at conception. The second type, which is called Post-birth Qi (Hou Tian Qi, 後天氣), is drawn from the Jing of our food and air. When this Qi flows or is led to the brain, it can energize the Shen and soul. This energized and raised Shen is able to lead the Qi to the entire body.

Each one of these three elements or treasures has its own root. You must know the roots so that you can strengthen and protect your three treasures.

1. Your body requires many kinds of Jing. Except for the Jing which you inherit from your parents, which is called Original Jing (Yuan Jing, 元精), all other Jings must be obtained from food and air. Among all of these Jings, Original Jing is the most important. It is the root and the seed of your life, and your basic strength. If your parents were strong and healthy, your Original Jing will be strong and healthy, and you will have a strong foundation on which to grow. The Chinese people believe that in order to stay healthy and live a long life, you must protect and maintain this Jing.

   The root of Original Jing before your birth was in your parents. After birth this Original Jing stays in its residence—the kidneys, which are considered the root of your Jing. When you keep this root strong, you will have sufficient Original Jing to supply to your body. Although you cannot increase the amount of Original Jing you have, Qigong training can improve the quality of your Jing. Qigong can also teach you how to convert your Jing into Original Qi more efficiently, and how to use this Qi effectively.

2. Qi is converted both from the Jing which you have inherited from your parents and from the Jing which you draw from your food and air. Qi that is converted from the Original Jing which you inherited is called Original Qi (Yuan Qi, 元氣).[11] Just as Original Jing is the most important type of Jing, Original Qi is the most important type of Qi. It is pure and of high quality, while the Qi from food and air may make your body too positive or too negative, depending on how and where you absorb it. When you retain and protect your Original Jing, you will be able to generate Original

Qi in a pure, continuous stream. As a Qigong practitioner, you must know how to convert your Original Jing into Original Qi in a smooth, steady stream.

Since your Original Qi comes from your Original Jing, they both have the kidneys for their root. When your kidneys are strong, the Original Jing is strong, and the Original Qi converted from this Original Jing will also be full and strong. This Qi resides in the Lower Dan Tian in your abdomen. Once you learn how to convert your Original Jing, you will be able to supply your body with all the Qi it needs.

3. Shen is the force which keeps you alive. It has no substance, but it gives expression and appearance to your Jing. Shen is also the control tower for the Qi. When your Shen is strong, your Qi is strong and you can lead it efficiently. The root of Shen (Spirit, 神) is your mind (Yi, or intention, 意). When your brain is energized and stimulated, your mind will be more aware and you will be able to concentrate more intensely. Also, your Shen will be raised. Advanced Qigong practitioners believe that your brain must always be sufficiently nourished by your Qi. It is the Qi which keeps your mind clear and concentrated. With an abundant Qi supply, the mind can be energized, and can raise the Shen and enhance your vitality.

The deeper levels of Qigong training include the conversion of Jing into Qi, which is then led to the brain to raise the Shen. This process is called "Huan Jing Bu Nao" and means "return the Jing to nourish the brain."[12] When Qi is led to the head, it stays at the Upper Dan Tian (center of forehead), which is the residence of your Shen. Qi and Shen are mutually related. When your Shen is weak, your Qi is weak, and your body will degenerate rapidly. Shen is the headquarters of Qi. Likewise, Qi supports the Shen, energizing it and keeping it sharp, clear, and strong. If the Qi in your body is weak, your Shen will also be weak.

1.7.2 Qigong Training Theory

In Qigong training it is important to understand the principle behind everything you are doing. The principle is the root of your practice, and it is this root which brings forth the results you want. The root gives life, while the branches and flowers (results) give only temporary beauty. If you keep the root, you can regrow. If you have just branches and flowers, they will die in a short time.

Every Qigong form or practice has its special purpose and theory. If you do not know the purpose and theory, you have lost the root (meaning) of the practice. Therefore, as a Qigong practitioner, you must continue to ponder and practice until you understand the root of every set or form.

Before you start training, you must first understand that all of the training originates in your mind. You must have a clear idea of what you are doing, and your mind must be calm, centered, and balanced. This also implies that your feeling, sensing, and judgment must be objective and accurate. This requires emotional balance and a clear mind, and requires a lot of hard work. But once you have reached this level you will have built the root of your physical training, and your Yi (mind) will be able to lead your Qi throughout your physical body.

As mentioned previously, Qigong training includes five important elements: regulating the body, regulating the breath, regulating the Yi (Mind), regulating the Qi, and regulating the Shen (Spirit). These are the foundation of successful Qigong practice. Without this foundation, your understanding of Qigong and your practice will remain superficial.

Regulating the Body (Tiao Shen, 調身)

Regulating the Body is called "Tiao Shen" in Chinese. This means to adjust your body until it is in the most comfortable and relaxed state. This implies that your body must be centered and balanced. If it is not, you will be tense and uneasy, and this will affect the judgment of your Yi and the circulation of your Qi. In Chinese medical society it is said: "(When) shape (body's posture) is not correct, then the Qi will not be smooth. (When) the Qi is not smooth, the Yi (Mind) will not be peaceful. (When) the Yi is not peaceful, then the Qi is disordered."[13] You should understand that the relaxation of your body originates with your Yi. Therefore, before you can relax your body, you must first relax or regulate your mind (Yi). This is called "Shen Xin Ping Heng," which means "Body and heart (Mind) balanced."[14] The body and the mind are mutually related. A relaxed and balanced body helps your Yi to relax and concentrate. When your Yi is at peace and can judge things accurately, your body will be centered, balanced, and relaxed.

Relaxation. Relaxation is one of the major keys to success in Qigong. You should remember that only when you are relaxed will all your Qi channels be open. In order to be relaxed, your Yi must first be relaxed and calm. When this Yi coordinates with your breathing, your body will be able to relax.

In Qigong practice there are three levels of relaxation. The first level is the external physical relaxation, or postural relaxation. This is a very superficial level, and almost anyone can reach it. It consists of adopting a comfortable stance and avoiding unnecessary strain in how you stand and move. The second level is the relaxation of the muscles and tendons. To do this your Yi must be directed deep into the muscles and tendons. This relaxation will help open your Qi channels, and will allow the Qi to sink and accumulate in the Lower Dan Tian.

The final stage is the relaxation which reaches the internal organs and the bone marrow. Remember, only if you can relax deep into your body will your mind be able to lead the Qi there. Only at this stage will the Qi be able to reach everywhere. Then you will feel transparent—as if your whole physical body had disappeared. If you can reach this level of relaxation, you will be able to communicate with your organs and use Qigong to adjust or regulate the Qi disorders which are giving you problems. You will also be able to protect your organs more effectively, and therefore slow down their degeneration.

Rooting. In all Qigong practice it is very important to be rooted. Being rooted means to be stable and in firm contact with the ground. If you want to push a car, you have to be rooted so the force you exert into the car will be balanced by a force into the ground. If you are not rooted, when you push the car you will only push yourself away, and not move the car. Your root is made up of your body's root, center, and balance.

Before you can develop your root, you must first relax and let your body "settle." As you relax, the tension in the various parts of your body will dissolve, and you will find a comfortable way to stand. You will stop fighting the ground to keep your body up, and will learn to rely on your body's structure to support itself. This lets the muscles relax even more. Since your body isn't struggling to stand, your Yi won't be pushing upward, and your body, mind, and Qi will all be able to sink. If you let dirty water sit quietly, the impurities will gradually settle down to the bottom, leaving the water above

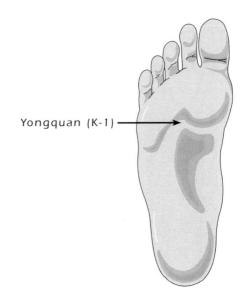

Yongquan (K-1)

Figure 1-1 The Yongquan Cavity (K-1)

it clear. In the same way, if you relax your body enough to let it settle, your Qi will sink to your Lower Dan Tian and the Bubbling Wells (Yongquan, K-1, 湧泉) at the center of the soles of the feet, and your mind will become clear (Figure 1-2). Then you can begin to develop your root.

To root your body you must imitate a tree and grow an invisible root under your feet. This will give you a firm root to keep you stable in your training. Your root must be wide as well as deep. Naturally, your Yi must grow first, because it is the Yi which leads the Qi. Your Yi must be able to lead the Qi to your feet, and be able to communicate with the ground. Only when your Yi can communicate with the ground will your Qi be able to grow beyond your feet and enter the ground to build the root. The Bubbling Well cavity is the gate which enables your Qi to communicate with the ground.

After you have gained your root, you must learn how to keep your center. A stable center will make your Qi develop evenly and uniformly. If you lose this center, your Qi will not be led evenly. In order to keep your body centered, you must first center your Yi, and then match your body to it. Only under these conditions will the Qigong forms you practice have their root. Your mental and physical center is the key which enables you to lead your Qi beyond your body.

Balance is the product of rooting and centering. Balance includes balancing the Qi and the physical body. It does not matter which aspect of balance you are dealing with, first you must balance your Yi, and only then can you balance your Qi and your physical body. If your Yi is balanced, it can help you to make accurate judgments, and therefore to correct the path of the Qi flow.

Rooting includes rooting not just the body, but also the form or movement. The root of any form or movement is found in its purpose or principle. For example, in certain Qigong exercises you want to lead the Qi to your palms. In order to do this you must imagine that you are pushing an object forward while keeping your muscles relaxed. In this exercise, your elbows must be down to build the sense of root for the push. If you raise the elbows, you lose the sense of "intention" of the movement, because the push would be ineffective if you were pushing something for real. Since the intention or purpose of the movement is its reason for being, you now have a purposeless movement, and you have no reason to lead Qi in any particular way. Therefore, in this case, the elbow is the root of the movement.

Regulating the Breath (Tiao Xi, 調息)

Regulating the breath means to regulate your breathing until it is calm, smooth, and peaceful. Only when you have reached this point will you be able to make the breathing deep, slender, long, and soft, which is required for successful Qigong practice.

Breathing is affected by your emotions. For example, when you are angry you exhale longer and more strongly than you inhale. When you are sad, you inhale longer and more strongly than you exhale. When your mind is peaceful and calm, your inhalation and exhalation are relatively equal. In order to keep your breathing calm, peaceful, and steady, your mind and emotions must first be calm and neutral. Therefore, in order to regulate your breathing, you must first regulate your mind.

The other side of the coin is that you can use your breathing to control your Yi. When your breathing is uniform, it is as if you were hypnotizing your Yi, which helps to calm it. You can see that Yi and breathing are interdependent, and that they cooperate with each other. Deep and calm breathing relaxes you and keeps your mind clear. It fills your lungs with plenty of air, so that your brain and entire body have an adequate supply of oxygen. In addition, deep and complete breathing enables the diaphragm to move up and down, which massages and stimulates the internal organs. For this reason, deep breathing exercises are also called "internal organ exercises."

Deep and complete breathing does not mean that you inhale and exhale to the maximum. This would cause the lungs and the surrounding muscles to tense up, which in turn would keep the air from circulating freely, and hinder the absorption of oxygen. Without enough oxygen, your mind becomes scattered, and the rest of your body tenses up. In correct breathing, you inhale and exhale to about 70% or 80% of capacity, so that your lungs stay relaxed.

You can conduct an easy experiment. Inhale deeply so that your lungs are completely full, and time how long you can hold your breath. Then try inhaling to only about 70% of your capacity, and see how long you can hold your breath. You will find that with the latter method you can last much longer than with the first one. This is simply because the lungs and the surrounding muscles are relaxed. When they are relaxed, the rest of your body and your mind can also relax, which significantly decreases your need for oxygen. Therefore, when you regulate your breathing, the first priority is to keep your lungs relaxed and calm.

When training, your mind must first be calm so that your breathing can be regulated. When the breathing is regulated, your mind is able to reach a higher level of calmness. This calmness can again help you to regulate the breathing, until your mind is deep. After you have trained for a long time, your breathing will be full and slender, and your mind will be very clear. It is said: "Xin Xi Xiang Yi," which means "Heart (Mind) and breathing (are) mutually dependent."[15] When you reach this meditative state, your heartbeat slows down, and your mind is very clear: you have entered the sphere of real meditation.

An Ancient Daoist named Li, Qing-An (李清庵) said: "Regulating breathing means to regulate the real breathing until (you) stop."[16] This means that correct regulating means not regulating. In other words, although you start by consciously regulating your breath, you must get to the point where the regulating happens naturally, and you no longer have to think about it. When you breathe, if you concentrate your mind on your breathing, then it is not true regulating, because the Qi in your lungs will become stagnant. When you reach the level of true regulating, you don't have to pay attention to it, and you can use your mind efficiently to lead the Qi. Remember where the Yi is, there is the Qi. If the Yi stops in one spot, the Qi will be stagnant. It is the Yi which leads the Qi and makes it move. Therefore, when you are in a state of correct breath regulation, your mind is free. There is no sound, stagnation, urgency, or hesitation, and you can finally be calm and peaceful.

You can see that when the breath is regulated correctly, the Qi will also be regulated. They are mutually related and cannot be separated. This idea is explained frequently in Daoist literature. The Daoist Guang Cheng Zi said: "One exhale, the Earth Qi rises; one inhale, the Heaven Qi descends; real man's (meaning one who has attained the real Dao) repeated breathing at the navel, then my real Qi is naturally connected."[17] This means that when you breathe you should move your abdomen, as if you were breathing from your navel. The earth Qi is the negative (Yin) energy from your kidneys, and the sky Qi is the positive (Yang) energy which comes from the food you eat and the air you breathe. When you breathe from the navel, these two Qi's will connect and combine. Some people think that they know what Qi is, but they really don't. Once you connect the two Qi's, you will know what the "real" Qi is, and you may become a "real" man, which means to attain the Dao.

The Daoist book *Chang Dao Zhen Yan (Sing (of the) Dao (with) Real Words)* says: "One exhale one inhale to communicate Qi's function, one movement one calmness is the same as (i.e., is the source of) creation and variation."[18] The first part of this statement again implies that the functioning of Qi is connected with the breathing. The second part of this sentence means that all creation and variation come from the interaction of movement (Yang) and calmness (Yin). *Huang Ting Jing (Yellow Yard Classic)* says: "Breathe Original Qi to seek immortality."[19] In China, the traditional Daoists wore yellow robes, and they meditated in a "yard" or hall. This sentence means that in order to reach the goal of immortality, you must seek to find and understand the Original Qi which comes from the Lower Dan Tian through correct breathing.

Moreover, the Daoist Wu Zhen Ren said: "Use the post-birth breathing to look for the real person's (i.e., the immortal's) breathing place."[20] In this sentence it is clear that in order to locate the immortal breathing place (the Lower Dan Tian), you must rely on and know how to regulate your post-birth, or natural, breathing. Through regulating your post-birth breathing you will gradually be able to locate the residence of the Qi (the Lower Dan Tian), and eventually you will be able to use your Lower Dan Tian to breathe like the immortal Daoists. Finally, in the Daoist song *Ling Yuan Da Dao Ge* (*The Great Daoist Song of the Spirit's Origin*) it is said: "The Originals (Original Jing, Qi, and Shen) are internally transported peacefully, so that you can become real (immortal); (if you) depend (only) on external breathing (you) will not reach the end (goal)."[21] From this song, you can see that internal breathing (breathing at the Lower Dan Tian) is the key to training your three treasures and finally reaching immortality. However, you must first know how to regulate your external breathing correctly.

All of these emphasize the importance of breathing. There are eight key words for air breathing which a Qigong practitioner should follow during his practice. Once you understand them you will be able to substantially shorten the time needed to reach your Qigong goals. These eight key words are: 1. Calm (Jing, 靜); 2. Slender (Xi, 細); 3. Deep (Shen, 深); 4. Long (Chang, 長); 5. Continuous (You, 悠); 6. Uniform (Yun, 勻); 7. Slow (Huan, 緩), and 8. Soft (Mian, 綿). These key words are self-explanatory, and with a little thought you should be able to understand them.

Regulating the Mind (Tiao Xin) 調心

It is said in Daoist society that: "(When) large Dao is taught, first stop thought; when thought is not stopped, (the lessons are) in vain."[22] This means that when you first practice Qigong, the most difficult training is to stop your thinking. The final goal for your mind is "the thought of no thought."[23] Your mind does not think of the past, the present, or the future. Your mind is completely separated from influences of the present such as worry, happiness, and sadness. Then your mind can be calm and steady, and can finally gain peace. Only when you are in the state of "the thought of no thought" will you be relaxed and able to sense calmly and accurately.

Regulating your mind means using your consciousness to stop the activity in your mind in order to set it free from the bondage of ideas, emotion, and conscious thought. When you reach this level your mind will be calm, peaceful, empty, and light. Then your mind has really reached the goal of relaxation. Only when you reach this stage will you be able to relax deep into your marrow and internal organs. Only then will your mind be clear enough to see (feel) the internal Qi circulation and to communicate with your Qi and organs. In Daoist society it is called "Nei Shi Gongfu," which means the Gongfu of internal vision.[24]

When you reach this real relaxation you may be able to sense the different elements which make up your body: solid matter, liquids, gases, energy, and spirit. You may even be able to see or feel the different colors that are associated with your five organs—green (liver), white (lungs), black (kidneys), yellow (spleen), and red (heart).

Once your mind is relaxed and regulated and you can sense your internal organs, you may decide to study the five element theory. This is a very profound subject, and it is sometimes interpreted differently by Oriental physicians and Qigong practitioners. When understood properly, it can give you a method of analyzing the interrelationships between your organs, and help you devise ways to correct imbalances.

For example, the lungs correspond to the element Metal, and the heart to the element Fire. Metal (the lungs) can be used to adjust the heat of the Fire (the heart), because metal can take a large quantity of heat away from fire, (and thus cool down the heart). When you feel uneasy or have heartburn (excess fire in the heart), you may use deep breathing to calm down the uneasy emotions or cool off the heartburn.

Naturally, it will take a lot of practice to reach this level. In the beginning, you should not have any ideas or intentions, because they will make it harder for your mind to relax and empty itself of thoughts. Once you are in a state of "no thought," place your attention on your Lower Dan Tian. It is said "Yi Shou Dan Tian," which means "The mind is kept on the Dan Tian."[25] The Lower Dan Tian is the origin and residence of your Qi. Your mind can build up the Qi here (start the fire, Qi Huo, 起火), then lead the Qi anywhere you wish, and finally lead the Qi back to its residence. When your mind is on the Lower Dan Tian, your Qi will always have a root. When you keep this root, your Qi will be strong and full, and it will go where you want it to. You can see that when you practice Qigong, your mind cannot be completely empty and relaxed. You must find the firmness within the relaxation, then you can reach your goal.

In Qigong training, it is said: "Use your Yi (Mind) to lead your Qi" (Yi Yi Yin Qi).[26] Notice the word lead. Qi behaves like water—it cannot be pushed, but it can be led. When Qi is led, it will flow smoothly and without stagnation. When it is pushed, it will flood and enter the wrong paths. Remember, wherever your Yi goes first, the Qi will naturally follow. For example, if you intend to lift an object, this intention is your Yi. This Yi will lead the Qi to the arms to energize the physical muscles, and then the object can be lifted.

It is said: "Your Yi cannot be on your Qi. Once your Yi is on your Qi, the Qi is stagnant."[27] When you want to walk from one spot to another, you must first mobilize your intention and direct it to the goal, then your body will follow. The mind must always be ahead of the body. If your mind stays on your body, you will not be able to move.

In Qigong training, the first thing is to know what Qi is. If you do not know what Qi is, how will you be able to lead it? Once you know what Qi is and experience it, then your Yi will have something to lead. The next thing in Qigong training is knowing how your Yi communicates with your Qi. That means that your Yi should be able to sense and feel the Qi flow and understand how strong and smooth it is. In Taiji Qigong society, it is commonly said that your

Yi must "listen" to your Qi and "understand" it. Listen means to pay careful attention to what you sense and feel. The more you pay attention, the better you will be able to understand. Only after you understand the Qi situation will your Yi be able to set up the strategy. In Qigong your mind or Yi must generate the idea (visualize your intention), which is like an order to your Qi to complete a certain mission.

The more your Yi communicates with your Qi, the more efficiently the Qi can be led. For this reason, as a Qigong beginner you must first learn about Yi and Qi, and also learn how to help them communicate efficiently. Yi is the key in Qigong practice. Without this Yi you would not be able to lead your Qi, let alone build up the strength of the Qi or circulate it throughout your entire body.

Remember when the Yi is strong, the Qi is strong, and when the Yi is weak, the Qi is weak. Therefore, the first step of Qigong training is to develop your Yi. The first secret of a strong Yi is calmness. When you are calm, you can see things clearly and not be disturbed by surrounding distractions. With your mind calm, you will be able to concentrate.

Confucius said: "First you must be calm, then your mind can be steady. Once your mind is steady, then you are at peace. Only when you are at peace are you able to think and finally gain."[28] This procedure is also applied in meditation or Qigong exercise: First calm, then steady, peace, think, and finally gain. When you practice Qigong, first you must learn to be emotionally calm. Once calm, you will be able to see what you want and firm your mind (steady). This firm and steady mind is your intention or Yi (it is how your Yi is generated). Only after you know what you really want will your mind gain peace and be able to relax emotionally and physically. Once you have reached this step, you must then concentrate or think in order to execute your intention. Under this thoughtful and concentrated mind, your Qi will follow and you will be able to gain what you wish.

Regulating the Qi (Tiao Qi) 調氣

Before you can regulate your Qi you must first regulate your body, breath, and mind. If you compare your body to a battlefield, then your mind is like the general who generates ideas and controls the situation, and your breathing is the strategy. Your Qi is like the soldiers who are led to the most advantageous places on the battlefield. All four elements are necessary, and all four must be coordinated with each other if you are to win the war against sickness and aging.

If you want to arrange your soldiers most effectively for battle, you must know which area of the battlefield is most important, and where you are weakest (where your Qi is deficient) and need to send reinforcements. If you have more soldiers than you need in one area (excessive Qi), then you can send them somewhere else where the ranks are thin. As a general, you must also know how many soldiers are available for the battle, and how many you will need for protecting yourself and your headquarters. To be successful, not only do you need good strategy (breathing), but you also need to communicate and understand the situation effectively with your troops, or all of your strategy will be in vain. When your Yi (the general) knows how to regulate the body (knows the battlefield), how to regulate the breathing (set up the strategy), and how to effectively regulate the Qi (direct your soldiers), you will be able to reach the final goal of Qigong training.

In order to regulate your Qi so that it moves smoothly in the correct paths, you need more than just efficient Yi-Qi communication. You also need to know how to generate Qi. If you do not have enough Qi in your body, how can you regulate it? In a battle, if you do not have enough soldiers to set up your strategy, you have already lost.

When you practice Qigong, you must first train to make your Qi flow naturally and smoothly. There are some Qigong exercises in which you intentionally hold your Yi, and thus hold your Qi, in a specific area. As a beginner, however, you should first learn how to make the Qi flow smoothly instead of building a Qi dam, which is commonly done in external martial Qigong training.

In order to make Qi flow naturally and smoothly, your Yi must first be relaxed. Only when your Yi is relaxed will your body be relaxed and the Qi channels open for the Qi to circulate. Then you must coordinate your Qi flow with your breathing. Breathing regularly and calmly will make your Yi calm, and allow your body to relax even more.

Regulating Spirit (Tiao Shen) 調神

There is one thing that is more important than anything else in a battle, and that is fighting spirit. You may have the best general, who knows the battlefield well and is also an expert strategist, but if his soldiers do not have a high fighting spirit (morale), he might still lose. Remember, spirit is the center and root of a fight. When you keep this center, one soldier can be equal to ten soldiers. When his spirit is high, a soldier will obey his orders accurately and willingly, and his general will be able to control the situation efficiently. In a battle, in order for a soldier to have this kind of morale, he must know why he is fighting, how to fight, and what he can expect after the fight. Under these conditions, he will know what he is doing and why, and this understanding will raise up his spirit, strengthen his will, and increase his patience and endurance.

It is the same with Qigong training. In order to reach the final goal of Qigong you must have three fundamental spiritual roots: will, patience, and endurance.

Shen, which is the Chinese term for spirit, originates from the Yi (the general). When the Shen is strong, the Yi is firm. When the Yi is firm, the Shen will be steady and calm. The Shen is the mental part of a soldier. When the Shen is high, the Qi is strong and easily directed. When the Qi is strong, the Shen is also strong.

All of these training concepts and procedures are common to all Chinese Qigong, and you should also adhere to them when practicing Taijiquan. To reach a deep level of understanding and penetrate to the essence of any Qigong practice, you should always keep these five training criteria in mind and examine them for deeper levels of meaning. This is the only way to gain the real mental and physical health benefits from your training. Always remember that Taiji training is not just the forms. Your feelings and comprehension are the essential roots of the entire training. This Yin side of the training has no limit, and the deeper you understand, the more you will see that there is to know.

1.8 Taijiquan and Qigong

The previous discussion can be summarized as follows:

1. Taiji was originally created as a martial arts style, and was used in combat. Qigong training was necessary for reaching the highest levels of fighting ability.

2. Taiji Qigong is only one style of martial Qigong, and martial Qigong is only one category of Chinese Qigong. Many of the Taiji Qigong movements were adapted from Taijiquan forms.

3. Taiji Qigong is different from many other martial Qigong systems in that it emphasizes the soft and builds up Qi internally through Nei Dan practice, although it also practices Wai Dan through the soft body movements. This is different from many other martial Qigong styles which are relatively harder physically and emphasize Wai Dan practice.

4. In the last fifty years, Taiji Qigong has been practiced mainly for health purposes, rather than martial ones.

Next, in order to understand Taiji Qigong, we should analyze the reasons for training.

1. **To help Taiji beginners feel their Qi.** Beginners usually do not have even the slightest concept of Qi. Taiji Qigong gradually gives them an understanding of Qi through feeling and experience. This kind of knowledge is necessary for any kind of advancement in Taiji. For this reason, Taiji beginners are usually taught some of the many simple Wai Dan forms.

2. **To teach Taiji beginners how to regulate the body, breathing, and Yi.** Once you have grasped the idea of Qi, you then start to learn how to regulate your body. This includes how to relax the body from the skin to as deep as the internal organs and bone marrow. Through this relaxation you are able to feel and sense your center, balance, and root. You must also learn how to regulate your breathing—normal abdominal breathing for relaxation and reverse abdominal breathing for Qi expansion and condensation. Most important of all, you must learn how to regulate your mind until it can be calm and concentrated without disturbance. All of these criteria are the critical keys to the correct practice of Taijiquan. If you start learning the Taiji

sequence without having already done this basic training, you will be preoccupied with the complicated movements, and will only be able to perform them in a superficial way.

3. **To teach Taiji beginners how to use their Yi to lead the Qi efficiently.** Once you have regulated your body, breathing, and mind, you will then be able to use your concentrated mind to lead the Qi to circulate smoothly and effectively.

4. **To teach Taiji practitioners how to circulate Qi in the 12 primary Qi channels and fill up the two main Qi vessels.** If you are able to use your mind to lead the Qi efficiently, you have completed the basic Taiji training. This is then the time for Taiji forms or sequence training. In addition, you should continue your Taiji Qigong training and learn how to build up your concentration to a higher level, and consequently build your Qi to a higher level. In addition, you should also learn how to increase the Qi in the two main vessels—the Yin Conception Vessel (Ren Mai, 任脈) and the Yang Governing Vessel (Du Mai, 督脈). Still meditation is normally used for this.

5. **To teach Taiji practitioners how to expand their Qi to the surface of the skin and to condense the Qi to the bone marrow.** When the body's Qi has been built to a higher level you then start learning how to lead the Qi to the skin to increase the skin's sensitivity and into the bones to nourish the marrow.

6. **To teach Taiji practitioners how to use the Qi to energize the muscles for maximum Jin manifestation.** When you are able to lead the Qi to the skin and condense it to the marrow efficiently, you can then use this Qi to energize the muscles to a high level. This is the secret to internal Jin (Nei Jin, 內勁). Internal Jin is the foundation and root of external Jin (Wai Jin, 外勁). If you are interested in knowing more about Taiji Jin, please refer to the author's book: *Tai Chi Theory and Martial Power*, available from YMAA Publication Center.

7. **To lead the advanced Taiji practitioner into the domain of spiritual cultivation.** The ultimate goal of Taiji Qigong practice is to lead you into the domain of emptiness where your whole being is in the Wuji (no extremity) state. When you have reached this goal, the Qi in your body and the Qi in nature will unite and become one, and all human desires will gradually disappear.

Although many Taiji masters have created Qigong forms, most of the training forms used today have been adopted from the Taiji sequence. For example, push, crane spreads its wings, wave hands in clouds, etc. are commonly used for Qigong training.

In order to understand why Taijiquan has become more popular than any other style of Qigong, you must first understand the differences between Taiji Qigong and most other Qigong systems:

1. Because Taijiquan was originally created for martial purposes, every movement has its defensive or offensive purpose. This means that the intention of the Yi must be strong in every movement. This enables the practitioner to lead the Qi more strongly and

efficiently to the limbs, internal organs, and marrow. Because of this heavy emphasis on Yi, the Qi flow can be more fluid, and the Qi can be increased more than with the usual Qigong practices that do not emphasize the Yi as strongly.

2. In order to manifest Taiji Jin (i.e., power) effectively and efficiently, the Jin must first be stored. Storing Jin (in the Yi, Qi, and posture) is Yin, while manifesting Jin is Yang. Taiji emphasizes the Yin side and the Yang side equally, and can consequently balance Yin and Yang in the body and avoid unhealthy extremes. This is different from many other Qigong practices which emphasize the Yang side more than the Yin side. Practitioners who emphasize the Yang training will not get sick easily, but, because their bodies become Yang, they will age more quickly than is normal.

3. Taiji Qigong includes both Nei Dan and Wai Dan training, and is more complete than those Qigong systems which emphasize only one or the other.

4. Taiji Qigong builds not only the Qi circulation in the primary Qi channels, but also the Guardian Qi in the skin (Yang) and the marrow Qi in the bones (Yin). In addition, Taiji Qigong also teaches the practitioner how to increase the level of Qi storage and circulation in the two major vessels—the Conception and Governing Vessels.

5. Taiji is soft, and does not use the muscular tension which most other martial Qigong styles use to some degree. Taiji Qigong emphasizes using the Yi to lead Qi in a relaxed body, and does not use tension to energize the muscles. This makes it easier for the practitioner to reach a calm, peaceful, meditative state. The practitioner is able to release mental stress and physical tension, and reach a higher level of relaxation. This is the key to maintaining and improving mental and physical health.

1.9 How to Use This Book

When you practice any Qigong, you must first ask: What, Why, and How. "What" means: "What am I looking for?" "What do I expect?" and "What should I do?" Then you must ask: "Why do I need it?" "Why does it work?" "Why must I do it this way instead of that way?" Finally, you must determine: "How does it work?" "How much have I advanced toward my goal?" And "How will I be able to advance further?"

It is very important to understand what you are practicing, and not just automatically repeat all that you have learned. Understanding is the root of any work. With understanding you will be able to know your goal. Once you know your goal, your mind can be firm and steady. With this understanding, you will be able to see why something has happened, and what the principles and theories behind it are. Without all of this, your work will be done blindly, and it will be a long and painful process. Only when you are sure what your goal is and why you need to reach it should you raise the question of how you are going to achieve it. The answers to all of these questions form the root of your practice, and will help you to avoid the wondering and confusion that uncertainty brings. If you keep this root, you will be able to apply the theory and make it grow—you will know how to create. Without this root, what you learn will be only branches and flowers, and in time they will wither.

In China there is a story about an old man who was able to change a piece of rock into gold. One day, a boy came to see him and asked for his help. The old man said: "Boy! What do you want? Gold? I can give you all of the gold you want." The boy replied: "No, Master, what I want is not your gold, what I want is the trick of how to change the rock into gold!" When you just have gold, you can spend it all and become poor again. If you have the trick of how to make gold, you will never be poor. For the same reason, when you learn Qigong you should learn the theory and principle behind it, not just the practice. Understanding theory and principle will not only shorten your time of pondering and practice, but also enable you to practice most efficiently.

One of the hardest parts of the training process is learning how to actually do the forms correctly. Every Qigong movement has its special meaning and purpose. In order to make sure your movements or forms are correct, it is best to work with the tape and book together. There are some important things which you may not be able to pick up from reading, but once you see them, they will be clear. An example is the transition movements between the forms. Naturally, there are other important ideas which are impossible to take the time to explain in the videotape, such as the theory and principles; these can only be explained in a book. It cannot be denied that under the tutelage of a master you can learn more quickly and perfectly than is possible using only tapes and books. What you are missing is the master's experience and feeling. However, if you ponder carefully and practice patiently and perseveringly, you will be able to make up for this lack through your own experience and practice. This book and tape are designed for self-instruction. You will find that they will serve you as a key to enter into the field of Qigong.

To conclude, you must practice with perseverance and patience. You need a strong will and a great deal of self-discipline. As mentioned earlier, you may find many different versions of Taiji Qigong taught by different masters. Do not be confused by all of these versions. You should understand that it does not matter which version you practice, the basic theory and principles remain the same. The most important thing is to build up the depth of your theoretical understanding so that your mind will be clear and you will understand where you are going.

References

1.　　專氣致柔。

2.　　莊子曰：〝真人之息以踵，眾人之息以喉。

3.　　人生七十古來稀。

4.　　安天樂命。

5.　　修身俟命。

6.　　一百二十謂之天。

7.　　There are many reports in popular and professional literature of using Qigong to help or even cure many illnesses, including cancer. Many cases have been discussed in the Chinese Qigong journals. One book which describes the use of Qigong to cure cancer is *New Qigong for Preventing and Curing Cancer* (新氣功防治癌症), by Ye Ming (葉明), Chinese Yoga Publications, Taiwan, 1986.

8.　　南雷集王征南墓誌銘：〝宋之張三豐爲武當丹士。徽宗召之，路梗不得進。夜夢元帝授之拳法，厥明以單丁殺賊百餘。〞

9.　　明史方妓傳：〝張三豐遼東懿州人，名全一。一名君寶。三豐其號也。以不修邊幅，又號張邋遢。頎而偉，龜形鶴背。大耳圓目，鬚髯如戟。寒暑惟一衲蓑，所啖升斗輒盡。或數日不食，或數月不食，一日千里。善嬉戲，旁若無人。嘗與其徒遊武當。築草廬而居之，洪武二十四年，太祖聞其名，遣使覓之不得。〞

10.　明郎瑛七修類稿：〝張仙名君寶，字全一。別號玄玄，時人又稱張邋遢。天順三年，曾來謁帝。予見其像，鬚鬢豎立，一髻背垂，紫面大腹，而攜笠者。上爲錫誥之文，封爲通微顯化眞人。〞

11. Before birth you have no Qi of your own, but rather you use your mother's Qi. When you are born, you start creating Qi from the Original Jing which you received from your parents. This Qi is called Pre-birth Qi, as well as Original Qi. It is also called Pre-heaven Qi (Xian Tian Qi) because it comes from the Original Jing which you received before you saw the heavens (which here means the sky), i.e. before your birth.

12.　　還精補腦。

13.　　形不正，則氣不順。氣不順，則意不寧。意不寧，則氣散亂。

14. 身心平衡。

15. 心息相依。

16. 調息要調無息息。

17.　　廣成子曰：〝一呼則地氣上升，一吸則天氣下降，人之反覆呼吸於蒂，則我之真氣自然相接。〞

18. 唱道眞言曰：〝一呼一吸通乎氣機，一動一靜同乎造化。〞

19. 黃庭經曰：〝呼吸元氣以求仙。〞

20. 伍眞人曰：〝用後天之呼吸，尋眞人呼吸處。〞

21. 靈源大道歌：〝元和內運即成眞，呼吸外求終未了。〞

22. 大道教人先止念，念頭不住亦徒然。〞

23. 無念之念。

24. 內視功夫。

25. 意守丹田。

26. 以意引氣。

27. 意不在氣，在氣則滯。

28. 孔子曰：〝先靜爾後有定，定爾後能安，安爾後能慮，慮爾後能得。〞

CHAPTER 2

The Root of Taijiquan– Yin and Yang

太極拳之根 - 陰、陽

The theory of Yin and Yang is the root of Taijiquan, and the source from which it was created and formalized. The Qigong sets, which are an essential part of the practice of Taiji, are also based on this theory. It is therefore desirable to understand Yin-Yang theory so that you can have a clear concept of what you are trying to accomplish in your practice.

2.1 The Concept of Yin and Yang, Kan and Li

■ 2.1.1 YIN AND YANG (陰、陽)

The Chinese have long believed that the universe is made up of two opposing forces—Yin and Yang—which must balance each other. When these two forces begin to lose their balance, nature finds a way to re-balance them. If the imbalance is significant, disaster will occur. However, when these two forces combine and interact with each other smoothly and harmoniously, they manifest power and generate the millions of living things.

Yin and Yang theory is also applied to the three great natural powers: heaven, earth, and man. For example, if the Yin and Yang forces of heaven (i.e., energy which comes to us from the sky) are losing balance, there can be tornadoes, hurricanes, or other natural disasters. When the Yin and Yang forces loose their balance on earth, rivers can change their paths and earthquakes can occur. When the Yin and Yang forces in the human body lose their balance, sickness and even death can occur. Experience has shown that the Yin and Yang balance in man is affected by the Yin and Yang balances of the earth and heaven. Similarly, the Yin and Yang balance of the earth is influenced by the heaven's Yin and Yang. Therefore, if you wish to have a healthy body and live a long life, you need to know how to adjust your body's Yin and Yang, and how to coordinate your Qi with the Yin and Yang energy of heaven and earth. The study of Yin and Yang in the human body is the root of Chinese medicine and Qigong.

The Chinese have classified everything in the universe according to Yin and Yang. Even feelings, thoughts, strategy, and the spirit are covered. For example, female is Yin and male is Yang, night is Yin and day is Yang, weak is Yin and strong is Yang, backward is Yin and forward is Yang, sad is Yin and happy is Yang, defense is Yin and offense is Yang.

Practitioners of Chinese medicine and Qigong believe that they must seek to understand the Yin and Yang of nature and the human body before they can adjust and regulate the body's energy balance into a more harmonious state. Only then can health be maintained and the causes of sickness be corrected.

Now let us discuss how Yin and Yang are defined, and how the concept of Yin and Yang is applied to the Qi circulating in the human body. Many people, even some Qigong practitioners, are still confused by this. When it is said that Qi can be either Yin or Yang, it does not mean that there are two different kinds of Qi like male and female, fire and water, or positive and negative charges. Qi is energy, and energy itself does not have Yin and Yang. It is like the energy which is generated from the sparking of negative and positive charges. Charges have the potential of generating energy, but are not the energy itself.

When it is said that Qi is Yin or Yang, it means that the Qi is too strong or too weak for a particular circumstance. It is relative and not absolute. Naturally, this implies that the potential which generates the Qi is strong or weak. For example, the Qi from the sun is Yang Qi, and Qi from the moon is Yin Qi. This is because the sun's energy is Yang in comparison to Human Qi, while the moon's is Yin. In any discussion of energy where people are involved, Human Qi is used as the standard. People are always especially interested in what concerns them directly, so it is natural that we are interested primarily in Human Qi and tend to view all Qi from the perspective of human Qi. This is not unlike looking at the universe from the perspective of the Earth.

When we look at the Yin and Yang of Qi within and in regard to the human body, however, we must redefine our point of reference. For example, when a person is dead, his residual Human Qi (Gui Qi or ghost Qi, 鬼氣) is weak compared to a living person's. Therefore, the ghost's Qi is Yin while the living person's is Yang. When discussing Qi within the body, in the Lung channel for example, the reference point is the normal, healthy status of the Qi there. If the Qi is stronger than it is in the normal state, it is Yang, and, naturally, if it is weaker than this, it is Yin. There are twelve parts of the human body that are considered organs in Chinese medicine, six of them are Yin and six are Yang. The Yin organs are the Heart, Lungs, Kidneys, Liver, Spleen, and Pericardium, and the Yang organs are Large Intestine, Small Intestine, Stomach, Gall Bladder, Urinary Bladder, and Triple Burner. Generally speaking, the Qi level of the Yin organs is lower than that of the Yang organs. The Yin organs store Original Essence and process the Essence obtained from food and air, while the Yang organs handle digestion and excretion.

When the Qi in any of your organs is not in its normal state, you feel uncomfortable. If it is very much off from the normal state, the organ will start to malfunction and you may become sick. When this happens, the Qi in your entire body will also be affected and you will feel too Yang, perhaps feverish, or too Yin, such as the weakness after diarrhea.

Your body's Qi level is also affected by natural circumstances such as the weather, climate, and seasonal changes. Therefore, when the body's Qi level is classified, the reference point is the level which feels most comfortable for those particular circumstances. Naturally, each of us is a little bit different, and what feels best and most natural for one person may be a bit different from what is right for another person. That is why the doctor will usually ask "how do you feel?" It is according to your own standard that you are judged.

Breath is closely related to the state of your Qi, and therefore also considered Yin or Yang. When you exhale you expel air from your lungs, your mind moves outward, and the Qi around the body expands. In the Chinese martial arts, the exhale is generally used to expand the Qi to energize the muscles during an attack. Therefore, you can see that the exhale is Yang—it is expanding, offensive, and strong. Naturally, based on the same theory, the inhale is considered Yin.

Your breathing is closely related to your emotions. When you lose your temper, your breathing is short and fast, i.e. Yang. When you are sad, your body is more Yin, and you inhale more than you exhale in order to absorb the Qi from the air to balance the body's Yin and bring the body back into balance. When you are excited and happy your body is Yang, and your exhale is longer than your inhale to get rid of the excess Yang which is caused by the excitement.

As mentioned before, your mind is also closely related to your Qi. Therefore, when your Qi is Yang, your mind is usually also Yang (excited) and vice versa. The mind can also be classified according to the Qi which generated it. The mind (Yi, 意) which is generated from the calm and peaceful Qi obtained from Original Essence is considered Yin. The mind (Xin, 心) which originates with the food and air Essence is emotional, scattered, and excited, and it is considered Yang. The spirit, which is related to the Qi, can also be classified as Yang or Yin based on its origin.

Do not confuse Yin Qi and Yang Qi with Fire Qi and Water Qi. When the Yin and Yang of Qi are mentioned, it refers to the level of Qi according to some reference point. However, when Water and Fire Qi are mentioned, it refers to the quality of the Qi. If you are interested in reading more about the Yin and Yang of Qi, please refer to Dr. Yang's books: *The Root of Chinese Qigong* and *Muscle/Tendon Changing and Marrow/Brain Washing Chi Kung*.

■ **2.1.2 KAN AND LI** (坎、 離)

The terms Kan and Li occur frequently in Qigong documents. In the Eight Trigrams Kan represents "Water" while Li represents "Fire." However, the everyday terms for water and fire are also often used. Kan and Li training has long been of major importance to Qigong practitioners. In order to understand why, you must understand these two words, and the theory behind them.

First you should understand that though Kan-Li and Yin-Yang are related, Kan and Li are not Yin and Yang. Kan is Water, which is able to cool your body down and make it more Yin, while Li is Fire, which warms your body and makes it more Yang. Kan and Li are the methods or causes, while Yin and Yang are the results. When Kan and Li are adjusted or regulated correctly, Yin and Yang will be balanced and interact harmoniously.

Qigong practitioners believe that your body is always too Yang, unless you are sick or have not eaten for a long time, in which case your body may be more Yin. Since your body is always Yang, it is degenerating and burning out. It is believed that this is the cause of aging. If you are able to use Water to cool down your body, you will be able to slow down the degeneration process and thereby lengthen your life. This is the main reason why Chinese Qigong practitioners have been studying ways of improving the quality of the Water in their bodies, and of reducing the quantity of the Fire. I believe that as a Qigong practitioner you should always keep this subject at the top of your list for study and research. If you earnestly ponder and experiment, you will be able to grasp the trick of adjusting them.

If you want to learn how to adjust them, you must understand that Water and Fire mean many things in your body. The first concerns your Qi. Qi is classified as Fire or Water. When your Qi is not pure and causes your physical body to heat up and your mental/spiritual body to become unstable (Yang), it is classified as Fire Qi. The Qi which is pure and is able to cool both your physical and spiritual bodies (make them more Yin) is considered Water Qi. However, your body can never be purely Water. Water can cool down the Fire, but it must never totally quench it, because then you would be dead. It is also said that Fire Qi is able to agitate and stimulate the emotions, and from these emotions generate a "mind." This mind is called Xin (心), and is considered the Fire mind, Yang mind, or emotional mind. On the other hand, the mind that Water Qi generates is calm, steady, and wise. This mind is called Yi (意), and is considered to be the Water mind or wisdom mind. If your spirit is nourished by Fire Qi, although your spirit may be high, it will be scattered and confused (a Yang spirit). Naturally, if the spirit is nourished and raised up by Water Qi, it will be firm and steady (a Yin mind). When your Yi is able to govern your emotional Xin effectively, your will (strong emotional intention) can be firm.

You can see from this discussion that your Qi is the main cause of the Yin and Yang of your physical body, your mind, and your spirit. To regulate your body's Yin and Yang, you must learn how to regulate your body's Water and Fire Qi, but in order to do this efficiently you must know their sources.

Once you have grasped the concepts of Yin-Yang and Kan-Li, then you have to think about how to adjust Kan and Li so that you can balance the Yin and Yang in your body.

Theoretically, a Qigong practitioner would like to keep his body in a state of Yin-Yang balance, which means the "center" point of the Yin and Yang forces. This center point is commonly called "Wuji" (no extremities, 無極). It is believed that Wuji is the original, natural state where Yin and Yang are not distinguished. In the Wuji state, nature is peaceful and calm. In the Wuji state, all of the Yin and Yang forces have gradually combined harmoniously and disappeared. When this Wuji theory is applied to human beings, it is the final goal of Qigong practice where your mind is neutral and absolutely calm. The Wuji state makes it possible for you to find the origin of your life, and to combine your Qi with the Qi of nature.

The ultimate goal and purpose of Taiji Qigong and Taijiquan is to find this peaceful and natural state. In order to reach this goal, you must first understand your body's Yin and Yang so that you can balance them by adjusting your Kan and Li. Only when your Yin and Yang are balanced will you be able to find the center balance point, the Wuji state.

Theoretically, between the two extremes of Yin and Yang are millions of paths (i.e., different Kan and Li methods) which can lead you to the neutral center. This accounts for the hundreds of different styles of Qigong which have been created over the years. You can see that **the theory of Yin and Yang and the methods of Kan and Li are the root of training in all Chinese Qigong styles. Without this root, the essence of Qigong practice would be lost.**

2.2 Yin and Yang in Taijiquan

In Wang, Zong-Yue's Taiji Classic he states "What is Taiji? It is generated from Wuji and is a pivotal function of movement and stillness. It is the mother of Yin and Yang. When it moves, it divides. At rest it reunites."[1] According to Chinese Daoist scripture, the universe was initially without life. The world had just cooled down from its fiery creation and all was foggy and blurry, without differentiation or separation, with no extremities or ends. This state was called "Wuji" (literally "no extremity"). Later, the existing natural energy divided into two extremes, known as Yin and Yang. This polarity is called Taiji, which means "Grand Ultimate" or "Grand Extremity," and also means "Very Ultimate" or "Very Extreme." It is this initial separation which allows and causes all other separations and changes.

You can see from this explanation that Taiji (Grand Ultimate) is not Wuji. Taiji is produced from Wuji and is the mother of Yin and Yang. This means that Taiji is the process which is between Wuji and Yin and Yang. Then what is Taiji? **It is the hidden force which is able to lead Wuji into the division of Yin and Yang, and also to lead the divided Yin and Yang to the unity of Wuji.** In humans, this hidden force is Yi. Yi is intention and the motivation to action and calmness. Yi is the force which divides Wuji into Yin and Yang, and Yi is also the force which combines Yin and Yang into Wuji. When this hidden force is applied to natural Qi or

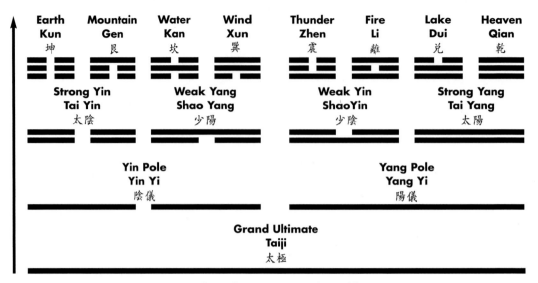

Figure 2-1. The Eight Trigrams are derived from Taiji

energy, it is the EMF (electromotive force) which is building up or diminishing. In one sense, Taiji is the first cause of Wuji and of the division into Yin and Yang.

When Yin and Yang theory is applied to man, its root of action is your Yi (wisdom mind). It is your mind which decides if you will change your Wuji state into the Yin and Yang state, or if you will lead yourself from Yin and Yang into Wuji. This means that your Yi is the EMF which determines the entire situation: your Yin and Yang strategy, actions, or the Qi movements in Taiji Qigong.

It is also said: "Taiji begets two poles, two poles produce four phases, four phases generate eight trigrams (gates), and eight trigrams initiate sixty-four hexagrams" (Figure 2-1). You can see that even Taiji is divided into Yin and Yang, that Yin or Yang themselves are again divided into Yin and Yang, and so on without end. For example, when Yin and Yang are divided in fighting strategy, each one must be subdivided into Yin and Yang, and each Yin and Yang must balance each other. The deeper you can analyze these layers and subdivisions of Yin and Yang and make them balance each other, the deeper you will be able to understand Taijiquan and Taiji Qigong.

Next, I would like to point out the basic Yin and Yang concepts in Taiji training. I hope this will help to give you a clearer understanding of the essence of Taiji, and thereby avoid errors and confusion in your training.

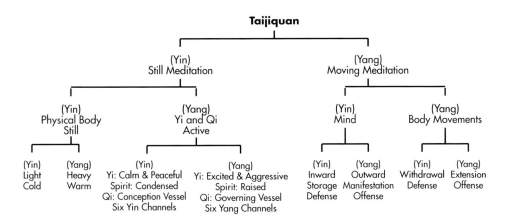

Figure 2-2. The Yin and Yang of Tai Chi

1. **TAIJI INCLUDES: a) STILL MEDITATION (YIN), AND b) MOVING MEDITATION (YANG)—FIGURE 2-2**

Yin still meditation can strengthen the mind (i.e., the EMF of the Qi), and can build up the Qi to a higher level. The still meditation of Taiji Qigong can open the paths of the Conception Vessel (Yin, 任脈) and Governing Vessel(Yang, 督脈), and increase the Qi stored in them. When the Qi in these two vessels is abundant, the Qi circulating in the twelve primary channels will be abundant, and therefore your physical body will be able to function more efficiently. Developing the Yi and the Qi through still meditation is the root of physical power. Remember: only when the Qi is strong can the power manifested by the physical body be strong. Qi is the Yin side of power, while the physical manifestation is the Yang side.

According to this theory, moving meditation is considered Yang because it manifests the Yi and Qi stored by Yin still meditation through the actions of the physical body.

The correct way of martial Taiji training is to practice both Yin still meditation and Yang moving physical manifestation equally. Many Taiji practitioners today ignore the Yin still meditation and practice only the external moving manifestation. They do not realize that building up the Yi and Qi is the key to effective Qigong and martial power (Jin, 勁) training.

Still meditation and moving meditation can also be divided into Yin and Yang:

a) Still Meditation includes: (1) The Stillness of the Body (Yin), and (2) The Activity of the Yi and Qi (Yang).

In still meditation, the physical body should be very still, relaxed, and calm. This opens the Qi channels and allows the Yi to lead the Qi strongly and without any stagnation. This stillness of the physical body is Yin. However, in order to build up the Qi and to circulate it strongly, the Yi must be strong and the Qi circulation must be alive and active. Therefore, the activity of the Yi and Qi is classified as Yang.

(1) **The Stillness of the Body includes: a) Light and Cold (Yin), and b) Heavy and Warm (Yang).**

During still meditation you will experience a different feeling. Normally, when you inhale, your physical body feels light and cold, and when you exhale, you feel heavy and warm. Naturally, all of these symptoms are closely related to the Qigong strategy, your breathing.

(2) **The Activity of the Yi and Qi includes: a) Yi is calm and peaceful, spirit is condensed (Yin), and b) Yi is excited and spirit is raised (Yang).**

When Yi is calm and peaceful, the spirit can be condensed and focused. The Qi circulates in the Conception Vessel and the six Yin channels, and it is condensed into the marrow and brain. However, when the Yi is excited and aggressive, then the spirit is raised. The Qi circulates in the Governing Vessel and the six Yang channels, and it expands to the skin.

b) **Moving Meditation includes: (1) Mind (Yin), and (2) Movement (Yang).**

In moving meditation, although the physical movements stimulate the body, the mind should remain calm so that it can lead the Qi smoothly and calmly. Therefore, the motion of the physical body is Yang and the calm mind is Yin.

(1) **Mind: a) Qi Condenses for Defense or Jin Storage (Yin), and b) Qi Expands for Attack (Yang).**

When your mind is on defending or on storing Jin for an attack, it will lead the Qi inward. The body will feel cold, and the Qi of the body will condense into the marrow; this mind is therefore classified as Yin. This condensing process is usually coordinated with inhalation in reverse abdominal breathing, and this inhalation is also classified as Yin.

However, when your mind is on an attack, it will lead Qi to the surface of the skin and to the limbs to energize the muscles to a higher level of efficiency. When this happens, the body feels warm and the energy of the body feels like it is expanding. Therefore, it is classified as Yang. Normally, this offensive process is coordinated with exhalation in reverse abdominal breathing, which is also classified as Yang.

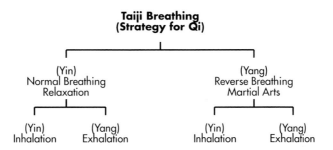

Figure 2-3. The Yin and Yang of Breathing

(2)   **Motion: a) Withdrawal and Defense (Yin), and b) Expansion and Offense (Yang).**

In the movement of Taijiquan, the withdrawing and defensive movements are Yin, while the expanding and offense movements are Yang. When you reach the level where the Yi, Qi, and movements are united, you have touched the essence of Taijiquan.

Naturally, the Yin defensive movements of Taiji can again be divided into Yin and Yang. For example, a completely defensive withdrawal movement is a Yin defense, whereas, if the withdrawal is used to set up an offense, it is considered a Yang defense. This is because the Yi stays Yang, even though the movement is Yin.

Similarly, in the Yang expanding, offensive movements, if the offensive movement is purely for striking, then it is Yang. However, if the offensive movement is used to set up for a retreat, the Yi is Yin, so the offensive movement is strategically Yin.

2.   TAIJI BREATHING INCLUDES: a) NORMAL BREATHING (YIN), AND b) REVERSE BREATHING (YANG)—FIGURE 2-3

Breathing is considered the strategy in Chinese Qigong. How you coordinate your breathing allows you to regulate your body and lead your Qi efficiently. There are two ways of breathing which are commonly used in Taiji. The first way is called "normal abdominal breathing" (Zheng Fu Hu Xi, 正腹呼吸), also sometimes called "Buddhist breathing," while the other way is called "reverse abdominal breathing" (Fan Fu Hu Xi, 反腹呼吸), also sometimes called "Daoist breathing." In normal abdominal breathing, when you inhale the abdomen (or Lower Dan Tian) expands, and when you exhale the abdomen withdraws. However, in reverse abdominal breathing the abdomen (or Lower Dan Tian) withdraws when you inhale, and expands when you exhale. It is usually easier to keep your body relaxed and feeling comfortable with normal abdominal breathing, so that is the method commonly used by those who practice Taiji only for health.

As for reverse abdominal breathing, many Taiji practitioners today falsely believe that the reverse breathing technique is against the way of the Dao. This is not true. It is simply used for different purposes. Try this simple experiment. Place one hand on your abdomen, and hold the other in front of you as if you were pushing something. Inhale deeply, and as you exhale, imagine that you are pushing a heavy object. You will easily see that, when you try to push as strongly as possible, you automatically use reverse breathing. This is the method which is commonly used in weightlifting competition. The competitors often wear a thick belt to support their abdomens and increase their power.

The rationale for reverse breathing is quite simple. You can lead a much stronger flow of Qi to the limbs and manifest more power if you also, simultaneously, direct another flow of Qi to your Lower Dan Tian. This is in accordance with the basic law of physics which states that for every action there must be an equal and opposite reaction. If you are still not convinced, try another experiment. Blow up a balloon, and hold a hand on your abdomen to see how it moves.

You can see from these experiments that reverse breathing is in accord with the Dao. It should be used whenever you need to lead Qi to the limbs to efficiently manifest power, as when you are fighting. Because it expands the Qi and energizes the body it is considered Yang in comparison to normal breathing.

a)   **Normal Breathing includes: (1) Inhalation (Yin), and (2) Exhalation (Yang).**

In normal breathing, inhalation is classified as Yin because the Qi is led from the limbs to the Lower Dan Tian, and exhalation is Yang because the Qi is led to the limbs.

b)   **Reverse Breathing includes: (1) Inhalation (Yin), and (1) Exhalation (Yang).**

Similarly, in reverse breathing, inhalation is classified as Yin because the Qi is led from the limbs to the Lower Dan Tian and from the skin to the bone marrow. Naturally, the exhalation is Yang because the Qi is led to the limbs from the Lower Dan Tian and to the skin from the bone marrow.

3.   TAIJI JIN INCLUDES: a) NEI JIN (YIN), AND b) WAI JIN (YANG); ALSO a) DEFENSIVE (YIN), AND b) OFFENSIVE (YANG)

There are two ways to classify the Yin and Yang of Taiji's Jin (power, 勁). The first way is according to how the Jin was generated, and the second way is according to the purpose of the Jin.

First, Taiji Jin can be classified as Nei Jin (Internal Jin, 內勁), which is Yin; and Wai Jin (External Jin, 外勁), which is Yang. Nei Jin training is the critical key which enables the Wai Jin to manifest its maximum power. Nei Jin includes how to build up the Qi to a higher level and how to lead Qi from the Lower Dan Tian to the limbs to energize the muscles. The mind is extremely important in Nei Jin training, and the methods are critical. The master usually does not reveal Nei Jin training to the student until he can be trusted.

Wai Jin concerns the physical movements of the Jin, which include the movement from the root of the stance, how to use the waist to direct the Jin from the legs to the limbs, and how to manifest and use the power. To use the analogy of a machine, Wai Jin is involved with how strongly the machine is built, while Nei Dan is concerned with the amount of energy which is put into the machine. Remember: the power and efficiency of the machine is determined by the energy supply.

Next, if we classify Jin according to its purpose, then the defensive Jin (Shou Jin, 守勁) is Yin while the offensive Jin (Fa Jin, 發勁) is Yang. Typical examples of defensive Jin are Listening Jin (Ting Jin, 聽勁), Yielding Jin (Zou Jin, 走勁), Leading Jin (Yin Jin, 引勁), and Neutralizing Jin (Hua Jin, 化勁). Typical examples of offensive Jin are Pushing Jin (Tui Jin, 推勁), Striking Jin (Da Jin, 打勁), Drilling Jin (Zuan Jin, 鑽勁), etc.

Jin can also be classified according to how the Jin is manifested. For example, Jin which relies more on muscles than Qi is classified as Hard Jin (Ying Jin, 硬勁)(Yang), while Jin which reduces the use of muscle to a very low level is classified as Soft Jin (Ruan Jin, 軟勁)(Yin). Naturally, like all other cases of Yin and Yang classification, these can be further sub-classified.

4. The Secret of Yin and Yang in Taiji practice

Kan-Li and Yin-Yang adjustments are critical keys for success in Qigong, and so adjusting them is one of the main subjects of both training and research. According to the experience of the last thousand years, a Nei Dan Qigong practitioner who wishes to adjust his Kan and Li efficiently must learn how to regulate his Yi and breathing. There are also several "Qiao Men" (Tricky Doors, 竅門) which have usually been kept secret, and only taught when the student had earned the trust of his master. One of the secrets is to touch the tongue to the roof of the mouth. This connects the Yin Conception Vessel to the Yang Governing Vessel. Without this, the Qi could stagnate in the mouth area and make the body too Yang.

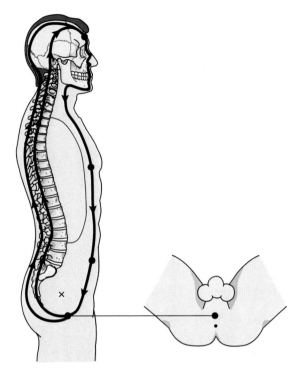

Figure 2-4. The Huiyin cavity

Another secret of Nei Dan training is using the Yi and the movement of the Huiyin cavity (Co-1, 會陰)(Figure 2-4) and the anus. When this is done in coordination with the correct breathing, it can effectively adjust the body's Yin and Yang. It is quite simple. If you use normal breathing, when you inhale and expand your abdomen you also gently expand your Huiyin and anus, and when you exhale and withdraw your abdomen you gently hold up your Huiyin and anus. It is important to know that holding up does not mean lifting up or tensing. Tensing causes Qi stagnation.

Practicing Taijiquan with normal breathing relaxes the body and mind and opens the twelve primary channels. This can effectively maintain your health. With normal breathing, when you inhale the Lower Dan Tian expands, you gently expand the Huiyin and anus, and at the same time use your Yi to lead the Qi to the bottom of your feet and further into the ground. However, when you exhale, the Lower Dan Tian withdraws, you gently hold up your Huiyin and anus, and at the same time use your Yi to lead the Qi upward to the Baihui (Gv-20, 百會). This is a calming and cleaning process which is used in almost all Qigong practices. Normal breathing and the coordination of the Huiyin and anus is the key to calming down both the physical and mental bodies, and it is one of the most effective ways of changing the body from Yang to Yin.

With reverse abdominal breathing you withdraw the abdomen and hold up the Huiyin and anus when you inhale, and expand the abdomen and gently expand your Huiyin and anus when you exhale. This enables you to energize the body and lead Qi out to the skin on the exhale, and lead Qi into the marrow and internal organs on the inhale. The inhale also leads Qi upward to your brain through the inside of your spine. If you do this right you will feel cold and light, and you may also experience a sense of rising. When you exhale this way you should feel hot, expanding, heavy, and sinking. You can see that inhaling is a way to become more Yin, while exhaling is a way to become more Yang. Inhalation is Kan while exhalation is Li.

In conclusion, when you practice Taiji Qigong it is important to remember to keep the tip of your tongue touching the center of the roof of your mouth. This must be done lightly, because if you exert too much pressure the tongue muscles will tense and stagnate the Qi circulation. In addition, you must remember that your Huiyin and anus must move up and down in coordination with your breathing. As always, your Yi remains the main key to successful Yin and Yang adjustment. Normal breathing is more effective in leading the Qi up and down, while reverse breathing is more efficient in leading the Qi inward and outward.

5. OTHER EXAMPLES

There are many other things in Taiji which are classified as Yin and Yang, but it would take too many pages to discuss them.

However, we will briefly discuss some typical examples. Once you understand the idea, you should be able to classify almost everything in Taiji into Yin and Yang.

1. The root is Yin and the limbs are Yang. In Taiji Jin, the power is generated from the legs, directed by the waist, and manifested by the limbs. The root is the origin of the power and is therefore Yin, and the limbs manifest this power and are therefore Yang.

2. Relaxation is Yin and tenseness is Yang. When you relax, your body and mind are calm and the Qi can be led into the organs and marrow. Relaxation is therefore Yin. When you are tense, the muscles are manifesting their strength and the power is demonstrated on the surface of the body, so tenseness is therefore Yang.

3. The center of the palm is Yin while the edge and fingers are Yang. In the palm, Qi is distributed from the Laogong cavity (P-8, 勞宮)(Figure 2-5) to the edge and to the fingers. Therefore, the center is Yin while the edge is Yang.

4. When the palms are facing up or forward, energy is emitted and so they are Yang. When they are facing toward your body or downward, the energy is conserved and they are Yin.

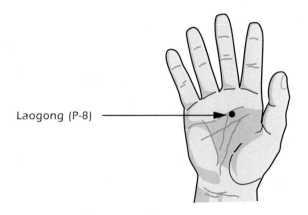

Figure 2-5. The Laogong cavity

5. Attack is Yang and defense is Yin. When you attack, the attacking hand is Yang and the rear leg which supports the attack is Yin. Also, if you grab the opponent's hand and pull, then the pulling hand is Yang while the front leg which is supporting the pull is Yin. Remember, Yin is the root, source, and cause of the power, while Yang is the power itself.

Again, every example of Yin and Yang can be subdivided into another Yin and Yang, and so on. The deeper you are able to dig, the more you will understand Taiji. This is the way to understand the essence and the root of Taijiquan.

References

1. 王宗岳：〝太極者，無極而生，動靜之機，陰陽之母也。動之則分，
   靜之則合。〞

CHAPTER 3

Taiji Qigong

太極氣功

3.1 General Training Concepts

Before we go into the practice of Taiji Qigong, you should understand a few things. First, if you look at your Qigong practice as a battle against sickness and aging, then your body is the battlefield, your mind is the general, your breathing is the strategy, your Qi is the soldiers, and your spirit is the morale of the general and soldiers. Therefore, in order to win this battle, you must know your battlefield (body) and learn how to arrange it most advantageously for the battle. The general (mind) who is in charge of the battle must be calm, wise, and always know what he is doing, so that he can set up the best strategy (breathing). When the battlefield, general, and strategy (body, mind, and breathing) are organized correctly, the soldiers (Qi) can be led effectively. You also need good fighting spirit and high morale.

When practicing Qigong, you should always pay attention to regulating your body, breathing, and mind. You must keep regulating them until your mind does not have to be on the regulating, and the regulation happens automatically. Then you will be able to feel the Qi, and your Yi will be able to lead it easily and smoothly. Ultimately, you will lead Qi to your head to nourish your brain and raise your spirit of vitality.

Second, although you can learn the theory and movements from this book, the movements will not be as alive and your understanding of them will not be as detailed as if you had learned them from an instructor. In other words, although a book can offer a detailed theoretical discussion which can ultimately lead you to a deep level of understanding, it is often unclear and misleading in its description of movement. A videotape can remedy this lack.

However, even if you have both book and videotape, you still will not get the feeling of the exercise. This internal feeling is one of the most important aspects of the exercise that an instructor can convey. However, despite all of these obstacles, thousands of Qigong practitioners have reached a high stage of practice through reading, pondering, and training. If you understand the theory, know the movements, and practice patiently and intelligently, then you can gradually accumulate enough experience to achieve a great depth of feeling for the exercise. Only when you have this feeling will you be able to say that you have gained the essence of the training.

Third, remember that theory is the Yin side of knowledge, while practice is the Yang side which manifests the theory. This means that if you really want to understand the exercise, you must both study the theory and practice the exercise. Each one helps the other, so that Yin and Yang can grow together and lead you to the essence of the practice. If you are interested in knowing more about Qigong theory, please refer to other YMAA Publication Center Qigong and Taiji publications.

In this chapter we will review the keys and the general concepts of successful Qigong training. Then we will introduce the warm-up Qigong. Beginners frequently ignore the warm-up Qigong training. This is unfortunate, because it is almost as important as the Qigong practice itself. The warm-ups prepare you by leading your mind and body into a deep meditative state where they are ready for the practice. You will then be able to feel and lead the Qi, which is critical for success. In other words, the warm-up Qigong is an integral part of the training.

3.2. Fundamental Training Principles

In this section we will summarize the training principles and rules which we have discussed earlier. During the course of your practice you should always keep them in mind.

Above all, understand your goal. For example, if you are only a beginner you should first learn to regulate your body until you feel relaxed and comfortable, and then begin regulating your breathing and mind. However, if you have practiced Qigong for a while and have already grasped the key points of regulating the body, breathing, and mind, you should then practice using the mind to lead the Qi. Naturally, if you have already reached this level, your target will be learning how to regulate your spirit. The process of regulation is crucial in Qigong, so let us review the procedures before we start discussing the actual training.

Regulating the Body (Tiao Shen) 調身. Regulating the body is adjusting your body until it is relaxed, centered, balanced, and rooted. For example, when you practice a pushing movement, the muscles should be relaxed to such a deep level that you can feel your arms relax all the way to the marrow. Only then can the Qi be led into the marrow and also to the surface of the skin. In addition, your movements must be coordinated with the movement of your torso. This enables your whole body to move smoothly and continuously as a unit. The coordination of the body enables you to find your balance. In every movement, your body must be upright (i.e., the head suspended) and rooted, and your pushing arm must also be rooted. For example, in a pushing movement your elbow must be sunk and your shoulder dropped. This allows you to find the root of the push, and makes it possible for your Yi to strongly lead your Qi. You can see that regulating the body is the most important and basic process in any Qigong practice.

Regulating the Breathing (Tiao Xi) 調息. When you have reached a level where you feel comfortable and natural and your body is relaxed, centered, rooted, and balanced, then the Qi circulation in your body will not be stagnant. In order to use your mind to lead the Qi efficiently, you must learn to regulate your breathing - which is the strategy of Qigong practice. If you breathe correctly, your mind will be able to lead your Qi effortlessly.

As discussed in the previous chapter, there are two common ways of breathing in Qigong: "Normal Abdominal Breathing" and "Reverse Abdominal Breathing." Normal Abdominal Breathing is commonly used to lead the Qi to circulate in the primary Qi channels. This helps you to relax both physically and mentally. However, if you wish to lead Qi to the surface of your skin and to the bone marrow, you would normally use Reverse Abdominal Breathing. It is more aggressive, and is therefore emphasized generally by martial Qigong practitioners.

Regardless of which breathing method you use, it is important to coordinate your breathing with the movements of your anus and Huiyin cavity. A more detailed discussion of these two breathing methods will be given later in this chapter.

Regulating the Mind (Tiao Xin) 調心. In regulating the mind, you first learn how to bring your mind and attention into your body. This is necessary for feeling the Qi circulation. The first step is learning how to control your emotional mind so that it is calm and peaceful and you can concentrate. Then you can use your Yi to lead your Qi.

Regulating the Qi (Tiao Qi) 調氣. Once you have learned how to use your Yi to lead your Qi effectively, then you can start working toward several goals in regulating your Qi. First, you want to make the Qi circulate smoothly and strongly in your body. Second, you want to build up the Qi to a higher level to strengthen your body. Third, you want to lead the Qi to the skin and also to the marrow. This will keep the skin fresh and young, and keep the blood factory (the marrow) functioning fully. Finally, you want to lead the Qi to your head to nourish your brain. It is the center of your whole being, and your health will have a firm root only if your brain is functioning well. If your brain is healthy, you can raise your spirit of vitality, which is the main key to the secret of longevity.

In order to reach these goals, you must first learn how to circulate the Qi in your body without any stagnation. This is possible when all of your concentration is on the Qi circulation, and there is no physical stiffness to make the Qi circulation stagnate. In time, it will feel like your physical body gradually disappears and becomes transparent.

Regulating the Spirit (Tiao Shen) 調神. Once you reach the stage of "transparency," you will be able to clearly feel the state of your body's Yin and Yang, and adjust them until you reach the state of Wuji (no extremity). When you have grasped this Wuji center, you will be able to return your whole spirit to its origin (the state before your birth), your Qi will unite with the Qi of nature, your spirit will unite with the spirit of nature, and you will become one with nature. This is the final goal of enlightenment and Buddhahood.

When you practice, you should also be aware of the following:

1. Do not practice when you are too full or too hungry.

2. Do not practice when you are upset. You will not be able to regulate your mind efficiently and may cause yourself harm, especially if you intend to use your Yi to lead your Qi.

3. Do not drink alcohol before practice. It can excite your emotions and Qi and make them unstable.

4. Do not smoke, since it will affect your lungs and the regulation of your breathing.

5. The best time to practice is just before sunrise. Eat a little bit right after you wake up in the morning, then practice about thirty minutes to one hour. If you would like to practice another time, the best time is two hours after dinner. The second practice in the evening will help you relax before sleep.

To conclude this section, always remember that the final goal of Taiji Qigong is to be natural. When you regulate your body, breathing, mind, Qi, and spirit, you should practice until the regulation happens naturally and automatically. This is the stage of "regulating without regulating." Only then will you be relaxed and comfortable, your Qigong practice effective and enjoyable.

3.3 Warm-Up Qigong

Before you start your Taijiquan or Taiji Qigong practice, you should always loosen up first to warm up your body. This will also prepare you mentally, so that you will get the best results.

In this section we will introduce some of the loosening up and warming up exercises which I have practiced for the last thirty-six years. Naturally, these exercises are only examples, and once you have practiced them and understand their theory and purpose, you may then create other movements which work better for you.

■ 3.3.1 Stretching the Trunk Muscles

Theoretically, the first place that should be stretched and loosened is the trunk muscles, rather than the limbs. The trunk is at the center of the whole body, and it contains the major

Figure 3-1

Figure 3-2

muscles which control the trunk and also surround the internal organs. When the trunk muscles are tense, the whole body will be tense and the internal organs will be compressed. This causes stagnation of the Qi circulation in the body and especially in the organs. For this reason, the trunk muscles should be stretched and loosened up before the limbs, and before any Qigong practice. Remember, people die from failure of the internal organs, rather than problems in the limbs. The best Qigong practice is to remove Qi stagnation and maintain smooth Qi circulation in the internal organs.

For these reasons, many Qigong practices start out with movements that stretch the trunk muscles. For example, in the Standing Eight Pieces of Brocade, the first piece stretches the trunk to loosen up the chest, stomach, and lower abdomen (which are the triple burners in Chinese medicine). In fact, this exercise is adapted from the Standing Eight Pieces of Brocade exercises.

First, interlock your fingers and lift your hands up over your head while imagining that you are pushing upward with your hands and pushing downward with your feet (Figure 3-1). Do not tense your muscles, because this will constrict your body and prevent you from stretching. If you do this stretch correctly, you will feel the muscles in your waist area tensing slightly because they are being pulled simultaneously from the top and the bottom. Next, use your mind to relax even more, and stretch out a little bit more. Stretch from the side ribs and back, rather than from just the shoulders. Also, be sure to keep the lower ribs in—don't let them hang

Figure 3-3

Figure 3-4

forward, as this will overarch your back. After you have stretched for about ten seconds, twist your upper body to one side to twist the trunk muscles (Figure 3-2). Stay to the side for three to five seconds, turn your body to face forward and then turn to the other side. Stay there for three to five seconds. Don't lose the up and down stretching of the torso, even while twisting. Repeat the upper body twisting three times, then tilt your upper body to the side and stay there for about three seconds (Figure 3-3), then tilt to the other side. Next, bend forward and touch your hands to the ground (Figure 3-4) and stay there for three to five seconds. Try not to round the back, which will put pressure on the internal organs. Finally, squat down with your feet flat on the ground to stretch your ankles (Figure 3-5), and then lift your heels up to stretch the toes (Figure 3-6). Repeat the entire process ten times. After you finish, the inside of your body should feel very comfortable and warm.

■ 3.3.2 WARMING UP
Loosening Up the Torso and Internal Organs

The torso is supported by the spine and the trunk muscles. Once you have stretched your trunk muscles, you can loosen up the torso. This also moves the muscles inside your body around, which moves and relaxes your internal organs. This, in turn, makes it possible for the Qi to circulate smoothly inside your body.

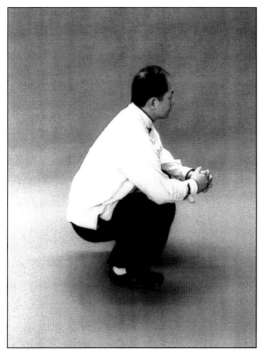

Figure 3-5

Figure 3-6

Abdomen

This exercise helps you to regain conscious control of the muscles in your abdomen. The Lower Dan Tian is the main residence of your Original Qi. The Qi in your Lower Dan Tian can be led easily only when your abdomen is loose and relaxed. The abdominal exercises are probably the most important of all the internal Qigong practices.

To practice this exercise, squat down in the Horse Stance. Without moving your thighs or upper body, use the waist muscles to move the abdomen around in a horizontal circle (Figure 3-7). Circle in one direction about ten times, and then in the other direction about ten times. If you hold one hand over your Lower Dan Tian and the other on your sacrum you may be able to focus your attention better on the area you want to control.

Figure 3-7

Figure 3-8

In the beginning you may have difficulty making your body move the way you want it to, but if you keep practicing you will quickly learn how to do it. Once you can do the movement comfortably, make the circles larger and larger. Naturally, this will cause the muscles to tense somewhat and inhibit the Qi flow, but the more you practice the sooner you will again be able to relax. After you have practiced for a while and can control your waist muscles easily, start making the circles smaller, and also start using your Yi to lead the Qi from the Lower Dan Tian to move in these circles. The final goal is to have only a slight physical movement, but a strong movement of Qi.

There are four major benefits to this abdominal exercise. First, when your Lower Dan Tian area is loose, the Qi can flow in and out easily. This is especially important for martial Taiji practitioners, who use the Lower Dan Tian as their main source of Qi. Second, when the abdominal area is loose, the Qi circulation in the large and small intestines will be smooth, and they will be able to absorb nutrients and eliminate waste. If your body does not eliminate effectively, the absorption of nutrients will be hindered, and you may become sick. Third, when the abdominal area is loose, the Qi in the kidneys will circulate smoothly and the Original Essence stored in the kidneys can be converted more efficiently into Qi. In addition, when the kidney area is loosened, the kidney Qi can be led downward and upward to nourish the entire body. Fourth, these exercises eliminate Qi stagnation in the lower back, healing and preventing lower back pain.

Diaphragm

Beneath your diaphragm is your stomach, on its right is your liver, and on its left is your spleen. Once you can comfortably do the movement in your lower abdomen, change the movement from horizontal to vertical, and extend it up to your diaphragm. The easiest way to loosen the area around the diaphragm is to use a wave-like motion between the perineum and the diaphragm (Figure 3-8). You may find it helpful when you practice this to place one hand on your Lower Dan Tian and your other hand above it with the thumb on the solar plexus. Use a forward and backward wave-like motion, flowing up to the diaphragm and down to the perineum and back. Practice ten times.

Figure 3-9

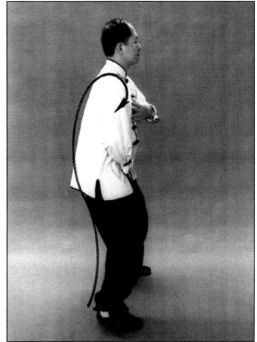

Figure 3-10

Next, continue the movement while turning your body slowly to one side and then to the other (Figure 3-9). This will slightly tense the muscles on one side and loosen them on the other, which will massage the internal organs. Repeat ten times.

This exercise loosens the muscles around the stomach, liver, gall bladder, and spleen, and therefore improves the Qi circulation there. It also trains you in using your mind to lead Qi from your Lower Dan Tian upward to the solar plexus area.

Chest

After loosening up the center portion of your body, extend the movement up to your chest. The wave-like movement starts in the abdomen, moves through the stomach and then up to the chest. You may find it easier to feel the movement if you hold one hand on your abdomen and the other lightly touching your chest (Figure 3-10). After you have done the movement ten times, extend the movement up to your shoulders (Figure 3-11). Inhale when you move your shoulders backward and exhale when you move them forward. The inhalation and exhalation should be as deep as possible, and the entire chest should be very loose. Repeat the motion ten times.

This exercise loosens up the chest and helps to regulate and improve the Qi circulation in the lungs. It also teaches martial Taiji practitioners to lead Qi to the shoulders in coordination

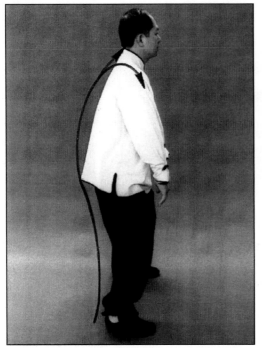

Figure 3-11

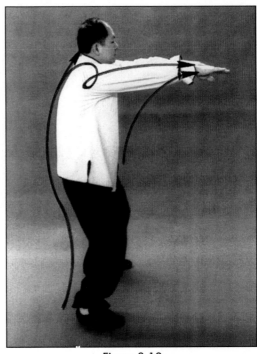

Figure 3-12

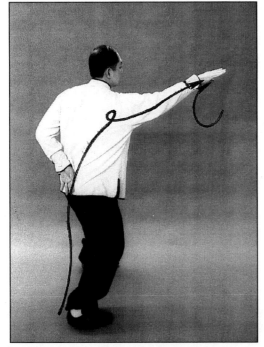

Figure 3-13

with the body's movements. In Taiji martial applications, Jin (power) is generated by the legs, directed by the waist, and manifested by the hands. In order to do this, your body from the waist to the hands must be soft and connected like a whip. Only then will there be no stagnation to hold back the power. If you are interested in reading more about Taiji Jin, please refer to the book *Tai Chi Theory and Martial Power,* by Dr. Yang.

Arms

Once you have completed loosening up the chest area, extend the motion to your arms and fingers. First practice the motion with both arms ten times, and then do each arm individually ten times. When you extend the movement to the arms you first generate the motion from the legs or the waist, and

Figure 3-14   Figure 3-15

direct this power upward. It passes through the chest and shoulders, and finally reaches the arms (Figure 3-12). When you practice with one arm, you also twist your body slightly to direct the movement to the arm (Figure 3-13).

These exercises will loosen up every joint in your body from the waist to the fingers. These exercises are in fact the fundamental practice of Jin manifestation in Taijiquan.

Once you have loosened up your body, you can work on specific areas with special movements. All of the following movements are part of the fundamental training for Taijiquan. You should practice each movement until it is smooth and natural and you can feel the Qi starting to flow following the pattern of the movements.

Rotating the Wrists

First, rotate both wrists at the same time. The motion is generated by the legs or waist, moves upward through the chest and arms, and finally reaches the wrists. Hold your arms out in front of you, and rotate both hands first inward ten times (Figure 3-14), and then outward ten times (Figure 3-15). Next, rotate each wrist individually ten times in one direction (Figure 3-16) and then ten times in the other direction (Figure 3-17). Again, the movement is generated from the waist or legs, so that as the wrist turns, the whole body is also moving to generate power for the wrist.

Figure 3-16

Figure 3-17

Figure 3-18

Coiling Forward and Backward

Now extend the motion so that you are coiling your arms. The motion is still generated from the legs or waist, is directed upward and passes through the chest and shoulders, and finally generates the coiling motion of the arms. Start with your hands in front of your chest with the palms facing downward (Figure 3-18), then coil both arms forward (Figure 3-19) and then backward (Figure 3-20). Repeat ten times. Remember to stay relaxed and to breathe smoothly, deeply and comfortably. Then coil the arms individually. Your right arm coils forward clockwise (Figures 3-21 and 3-22), and backward counterclockwise (Figures 3-23 and 3-24). The left arm coils counterclockwise forward and clockwise back. Exhale with the forward motion, and inhale when coiling your arm back. Do ten repetitions with each arm.

Figure 3-19

Figure 3-20

Figure 3-21

Figure 3-22

Figure 3-23   Figure 3-24

Settling the Wrists

This movement is used frequently in Taijiquan. Practice first with both hands, and then practice with each hand singly. Again, the movement starts with the legs or waist and is directed up to the wrists. To practice using both hands, hold your arms out in front of you, with the palms down and the fingers pointing forward (Figure 3-25). Generate a coiling motion with your legs or waist and, as the motion reaches the hands, lower your wrists so that the palms face forward and the motion becomes a push forward with the palms (Figure 3-26). When you practice single handed, you need to twist your body forward and backward slightly so that the pushing power can be directed to the pushing hand more efficiently (Figures 3-27 and 3-28). Practice the two hand press ten times and then each hand singly ten times.

Rotating the Ball

Rotating the ball is one of the most basic exercises to connect your upper body together so that it moves as a unit. Imagine that you are holding a basketball, and rotate it every which way in front of your chest. As always, the motion starts with the legs or waist (Figure 3-29). After rotating the ball about ten times in front of your chest, move the imaginary ball down to in front of your abdomen and rotate it about ten times there (Figure 3-30). There is no fixed pattern for rotating the ball. As long as your arms and body move as a unit and you maintain the

Figure 3-25

Figure 3-26

Figure 3-27

Figure 3-28

Figure 3-29   Figure 3-30

sense of holding a ball, you may rotate the ball any way you like. This exercise is an excellent way to thread the entire body together. A more complete explanation and several exercises for Taiji ball training will be discussed in the book *Taiji Ball Qigong* which YMAA intends to publish at a later date.

Pushing to the Sides

Hold your arms extended to the sides with the fingers pointing to the sides (Figure 3-31). Generate a feeling of motion from the legs or waist and direct it out to the arms. When the motion reaches the hands, settle (lower) your wrists and press to the sides with your palms (Figure 3-32).

Although these exercises are used as warm-ups, if you add your Yi (intention) to each movement you will feel a strong Qi flow. If you are using your Yi to lead your Qi in a relaxed movement, you are already doing Taijiquan. Remember that these warm-up exercises are offered only as suggestions. They can start you off on the correct path for Taijiquan or Taiji Qigong, but once you are familiar with them, you may combine them with exercises from other sources or even create exercises of your own.

Figure 3-31

Figure 3-32

3.4 Still Taiji Qigong

Taiji Qigong can be divided into two parts: the still meditative practice and the moving meditative practice. There are many different sets of moving patterns, each with its own unique purpose and benefits. We will discuss the still meditative practices in this section, and the moving ones in the next section.

Before we start, there are several important concepts which you should understand. As explained in the second chapter, compared with the moving Taijiquan which is classified as Yang, the still meditation is classified as Yin. Again, in Taiji still meditation, the sitting meditation is considered Yin, while the standing still meditation is considered Yang. In both cases the physical body is still, calm, and relaxed as much as possible, and therefore the body is classified as Yin, while the Qi generated and circulated in the Yin body is classified as Yang.

There are a number of other differences between sitting and standing still meditation. First, in the sitting meditation the physical body is relaxed to the maximum, while in the standing meditation the physical body is relatively tensed in certain areas. Second, sitting meditation builds up the Qi through Nei Dan (Internal Elixir, 內丹) training and completing the Small Circulation (Xiao Zhou Tian, 小周天), while the standing meditation builds up the Qi in the limbs through Wai Dan (External Elixir, 外丹) practice. In the sitting meditation, the Qi is built up in the Lower Dan Tian, which is the residence of Original Qi. It is located about one to two inches below the navel. The main goal of sitting meditation is to remove all blockages causing stagnation of the Qi flow in the Conception and Governing Vessels. However, the goal of standing still meditation is to build up the Qi by using certain postures which cause tension in specific muscles, energizing them and increasing their level of Qi. Therefore, in the Yin sitting meditation, the body and the mind are both calm, while in the Yang standing meditation, although the mind is calm, the physical body is excited to a degree. If you are interested in learning more about Nei Dan and Wai Dan Qigong, you should read Dr. Yang's book *Qigong for Health and Martial Arts*.

In this section we will discuss sitting still meditation for Small Circulation. However, if you are a Qigong beginner, we recommend that you do not start this training on your own. Nei Dan Qigong is hard to understand and experience, especially for Qigong beginners. If you do not understand the training theory and practice correctly, you may injure yourself. Wai Dan standing meditation is generally much safer. We are presenting the following discussion for your information, but you should wait until you understand Qigong and this training fairly well before you start the practice on your own.

■ 3.4.1 NEI DAN SITTING MEDITATION

Although Small Circulation is usually achieved through Nei Dan still meditation, there are several Wai Dan techniques which can also be used to achieve the same goal. These Wai Dan Small Circulation practices are normally done by martial artists in the Shaolin styles. For example, some of the Muscle/Tendon Changing (Yi Jin Jing, 易筋經) exercises are for Small Circulation. This subject is discussed in the book *Muscle/Tendon Changing and Marrow/Brain Washing Chi Kung*. There are many Nei Dan techniques for Small Circulation which the different Qigong styles have developed. In this book I will only introduce the one which I have practiced.

Small Circulation training has two major goals. The first is to circulate the Qi smoothly in the Conception and Governing Vessels. The second is to fill up the Qi in these two vessels.

We have explained earlier that there are eight vessels in the human body which behave like Qi reservoirs and regulate the Qi level in the twelve primary Qi channels. Among these eight vessels, the Conception Vessel is responsible for the six Yin channels, while the Governing Vessel controls the six Yang channels. In order to regulate the Qi in the twelve primary channels efficiently, the Qi in the vessels must be abundant. Also, the Qi in these two vessels must be able to circulate smoothly. If there is any stagnation of this Qi flow, the vessels will not be able to regulate the Qi in the channels effectively, and the organs will not be able to function normally.

You can see that Small Circulation is the first step in Nei Dan Qigong. Small Circulation training will help you to build up a firm foundation for further Nei Dan practices such as Grand Circulation and the Marrow/Brain Washing (Xi Sui Jing, 洗髓經).

In order to reach a deep stage of Nei Dan still meditation, it is especially critical that you follow the five important training procedures which we discussed earlier: a. regulating the body, b. regulating the breathing, c. regulating the mind, d. regulating the Qi, and e. regulating the spirit. You also need to know the location of the Lower Dan Tian and the roles which the Conception and Governing Vessels play in Qigong. These are discussed in detail in the author's Qigong book: *The Root of Chinese Qigong.* It is recommended that you study before you start practicing Small Circulation. Since Nei Dan Small Circulation has been discussed in detail in the author's earlier Qigong book: *Qigong for Health and Martial Arts,* we will only review the techniques here.

Abdominal Exercises

You start Small Circulation training by building up Qi at the Lower Dan Tian. This is done through abdominal exercises. You must first learn how to control the abdominal muscles again so that they can expand and withdraw. This exercise is called "Fan Tong" (Back to Childhood, 返童). From birth until about eight years of age, you move your abdomen in and out in coordination with your breathing. This abdominal movement was necessary for bringing nutrients and oxygen in through the umbilical cord when you were in the womb. However, once you were born, you started taking in food through your mouth and oxygen through your nose, and the abdominal movement gradually diminished. Most adults don't have this abdominal movement when they breathe. The "Back to Childhood" exercise helps you to return to this type of breathing.

Once you have regained control of your abdomen, if you continue these exercises you will feel your abdomen getting warm. This indicates that the Qi is accumulating. This is called "Qi Huo" (Starting the Fire, 起火). These exercises lead the Qi which has been converted from the Original Essence in the kidneys to the Lower Dan Tian, where it resides. The more you practice, the easier this is to do, and the more you can relax your body and feel the Qi.

Breathing

Breathing is considered the "strategy" in Qigong. In Small Circulation you may use either of the so called Buddhist or Daoist breathing strategies. Buddhist breathing is also called "Zheng Hu Xi" (normal breathing, 正呼吸) while Daoist breathing is called "Fan Hu Xi" (reverse breathing, 反呼吸). In Buddhist breathing, you expand your abdomen as you inhale and contract it as you exhale. Daoist Breathing is just the reverse (Figure 3-33).

As explained in the last chapter, Buddhist breathing is generally more relaxed than Daoist breathing. Although Daoist breathing is more tense and harder to train, it is more efficient in expanding the Guardian Qi (Wei Qi, 衛氣) and in martial applications. This point can be clarified if you pay attention to the everyday movements of your abdomen. Normally, if you are relaxed or not doing heavy work, you will notice that you are using Buddhist breathing. However, if you are doing heavy work and exerting a lot of force, for example pushing a car or lifting a heavy box, then you will find that your abdomen tenses and expands when you push

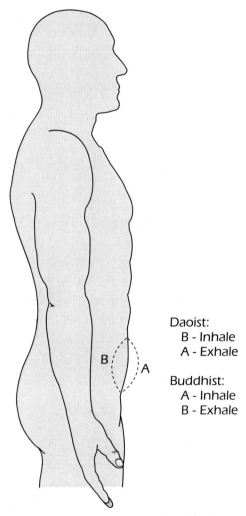

Daoist:
B - Inhale
A - Exhale

Buddhist:
A - Inhale
B - Exhale

Figure 3-33. Daoist and Buddhist breathing

or lift (which is Daoist breathing). It is suggested that beginners start with Buddhist breathing. After you have mastered it, you should then practice Daoist breathing. There is no conflict. After you practice for a while, you will find that you can switch from one to the other very easily.

Huiyin and Anus Coordination

After you have practiced the abdominal exercises for about three to five weeks, you may feel your abdomen get warmer every time you practice. After continued practice, the abdomen will start to tremble and shake each time you start the fire. This means that Qi has accumulated at the Lower Dan Tian and is about to overflow. At this time you should start to coordinate your breathing and abdominal movement with the movement of your Huiyin (Co-1, 會陰)(literally "Meet the Yin") cavity and anus to lead the Qi to the tailbone (Weilu cavity)(尾閭).

The technique is very simple. If you are doing the Buddhist breathing, every time you inhale, gently expand your Huiyin and anus, when you exhale you hold them up gently. If you are doing the Daoist breathing, the movement of the Huiyin and anus is reversed: when you inhale you gently hold them up and when you exhale, you gently push them out. This up and down practice with the anus is called "Song Gang" (鬆肛) and "Bi Gang" (閉肛)(loosen the anus and close the anus). When you move your Huiyin and anus, you must be relaxed and gentle, and must avoid all tension. If you tense them, the Qi will stagnate there and will not be able to flow smoothly.

The trick of holding up and loosening the Huiyin and anus is extremely important in Nei Dan Qigong. It is the first key to changing the body from Yin to Yang and from Yang to Yin. The bottom of your body is where the Conception (Yin) and Governing (Yang) Vessels meet. It is also the key to opening the first gate, which will be discussed next.

The Three Gates

There are three places along the course of the Small Circulation where the Qi is most commonly stagnant. Before you can fill up the Conception and Governing Vessels and circulate Qi smoothly, you must open these three gates, called "San Guan" (三關) in Chinese. The three gates are:

Tailbone

This cavity (Figure 3-34) is called "Weilu" (Tailbone, 尾閭) in Qigong and "Changqiang" (Gv-1) (Longstrength, 長強) in Chinese medicine.

Because there is only a thin layer of muscle on the tailbone, the Qi vessel there is narrow, and can easily be obstructed. Once you have built up a lot of Qi in the Lower Dan Tian and are ready to start circulating it, the tailbone cavity must be open, or the Qi might flow into the legs. Since you are only a beginner, you might not know how to lead the Qi back to its original path. If the Qi stagnates in the legs it could cause problems, perhaps even paralysis of the legs. This danger can be prevented if you sit with your legs crossed during meditation, which will narrow the Qi path from your Lower Dan Tian to the legs and prevent Qi from overflowing downward.

To prevent this kind of problem, you must know one of the important tricks which is called "Yi Yi Yin Qi" which means "use your Yi to lead your Qi."[1] Please pay attention to the word "lead." Qi behaves like water - it can be led, but it cannot be pushed. The more you intend to push Qi, the more you will tense, and the worse the Qi will circulate. Therefore, the trick is to always place your Yi ahead of your Qi. If you can catch this trick, you will find that the Qi can get through the tailbone cavity.

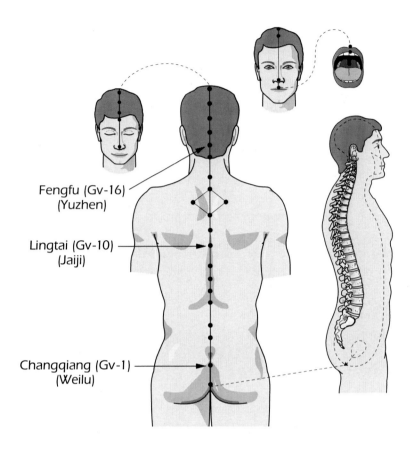

Figure 3-34. The Changqiang (Weilu), Lingtai (Jaiji), and Fengfu (Yuzhen) cavities

Because there are two big sets of muscles in the back beside the Governing Vessel, whenever there is extra Qi flowing through, these muscles will be slightly energized. The area will feel warm and slightly tense. Sometimes the area will feel slightly numb. All of these verify that Qi has been led to that point.

Squeeze the Spine

This cavity (Figure 3-34) is called "Jiaji" (夾脊)(Squeeze the Spine) in Qigong, "Mingmen" (Life Door, 命門) in the martial arts, and "Lingtai" (Gv-10)(Spirit's Platform) in acupuncture.

The Jiaji gate is located between the sixth and seventh thoracic vertebrae, behind the heart. If the Jiaji is blocked and you circulate Qi to it, part of the Qi will flow to the heart and overstimulate it. This will generally cause the heart to beat faster. If you become scared and pay attention to the heart, you are using your Yi to lead more Qi to it. This will make the situation worse.

The trick of leading Qi through this cavity is to not pay attention to your heart, though you should be aware of it. Instead, place your Yi a few inches above the Jiaji. Since Qi follows the Yi, the Qi will pass through without too much effort.

You can easily tell when the Qi is passing between the tailbone and the neck, because the muscles will feel numb, tense, or warm.

Jade Pillow

This cavity (Figure 3-34) is called "Yuzhen" (Jade Pillow, 玉枕) in Qigong and "Fengfu" (Gv-16) (Wind's Dwelling) in acupuncture.

The Jade Pillow cavity is the last gate which you must open. The cavity is so named because it is located in that part of your head which rests on the pillow, which the Chinese liked to make out of jade. There is not much muscle in this area, and so the path of the Governing Vessel is narrow, and easily constricted. This lack of muscle creates another problem. Because most of the spine is surrounded by layers of muscle, it is easy to gauge where the Qi is because of the response of the muscles. However, from the Jade Pillow up over the head there is very little muscle, and it is harder to tell what is happening with the Qi. This is especially confusing for beginners, but if you take it easy and proceed carefully, you will soon learn to recognize the new sensations. For some people, when the Qi passes through the Jade Pillow cavity it feels like insects walking over their heads. Other people feel numbness or itching.

Be very conscientious when you move Qi through this area. If you do not lead the Qi in the right path, the Qi may spread over your head. If it is not kept near the surface, it may enter your brain and affect your thinking. It is said that this can sometimes even cause permanent damage to the brain.

Breathing and Qi Circulation

In Qigong, breathing is considered your strategy. Although there is only one goal, there can be many strategies. It is the same as when you are playing chess with someone. Although you both have the same goal, and want to checkmate the opponent's king, there are many different ways you can go about it. Chinese Qigong has developed at least thirteen different strategies or methods of training. It is hard to say which is the best breathing strategy. It depends on the individual's understanding, the depth of his Qigong practice, and his training goals.

When you train using your breathing to lead the Qi, you should always pay attention to several things. The first is keeping the tip of your tongue touching the roof of your mouth (Figure 3-35). This connects the Yin (Conception) and Yang (Governing) Vessels. This process is called "Da Qiao" (搭橋), which means "building a bridge." It allows the Qi to circulate smoothly between the Yin and Yang vessels. The bridge also causes your mouth to generate

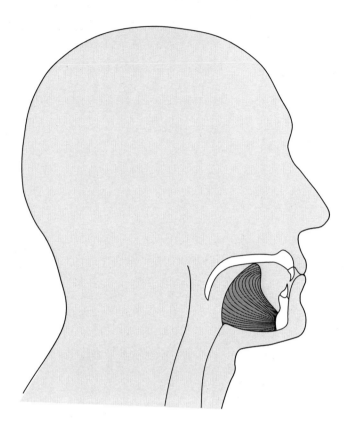

Figure 3-35. Tongue position in Qigong practice

saliva, which keeps your throat moist during meditation. The area beneath the tongue where saliva is generated is called "Tian Chi" (Heavenly Pond, 天池).

The second thing you need to pay attention to is the strength of your Yi, and how effectively it is leading the Qi. The third thing is how much your Shen is able to follow the breathing strategy. It is said: "Shen Xi Xiang Yi," which means "spirit and breathing mutually rely on each other."[2] As long as the Qi can be led effectively and the Shen can be raised strongly while the body is relaxed and the mind calm, the breathing strategy is having an effect.

We would like to recommend several breathing strategies which are commonly used to lead the Qi in training the Small Circulation.

Daoist Breathing Strategy

As discussed earlier, for much of their practices, Daoists use reverse breathing, whereby the abdomen draws in as you inhale, and expands as you exhale. This type of breathing reflects and augments the expanding and withdrawing of the Qi. As you exhale, the Qi can be expanded to the skin, the limbs, or even beyond the skin, while as you inhale the Qi can be drawn deep into

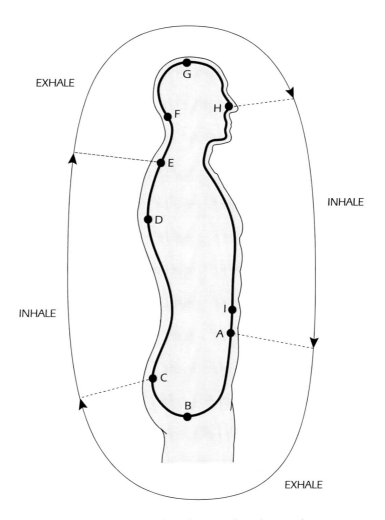

Figure 3-36. Two breath Daoist breathing cycle

the marrow. Reverse breathing is the natural way your body breathes when you want to get power out. Martial artists use this strategy of exhaling while the abdomen expands. The disadvantage of reverse breathing is that it is harder for beginners. When you do not do reverse breathing correctly, you will feel tension in your abdomen and a buildup of pressure in your solar plexus. This significantly affects the Qi circulation. To avoid this, it is highly recommended that Qigong beginners start with the so called Buddhist breathing. Only when breathing this way is easy, natural, and comfortable should you switch to the so-called Daoist reverse breathing.

There are two common ways to use the Daoist breathing to lead the Qi for Small Circulation, one with two inhalations and exhalations per cycle, and the other with one inhalation and exhalation per cycle.

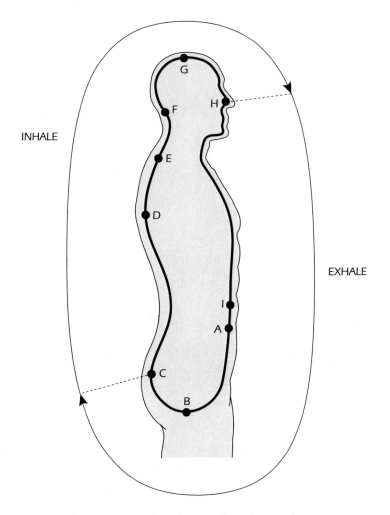

Figure 3-37. One breath Daoist breathing cycle

Two Breath Cycle (Figure 3-36). In your first inhale, lead the Qi to the Lower Dan Tian; when you exhale, lead the Qi from the Lower Dan Tian to the tailbone. As you inhale again, lead the Qi from the tailbone up along the spine to the level of the shoulders, and as you exhale, lead the Qi over the head to the nose to complete the cycle.

One Breath Cycle (Figure 3-37). On the exhale, lead the Qi from the nose to the tailbone, and on the inhale, lead the Qi from the tailbone to the nose to complete the cycle. In Daoist breathing, the inhalation is always used to lead Qi from the tailbone up the spine. If you try to do this with the exhalation, then you will be pushing the Qi, and not leading it.

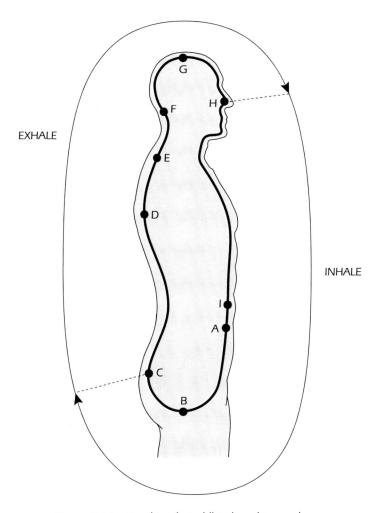

Figure 3-38. One breath Buddhist breathing cycle

Buddhist Breathing Strategy

The Buddhists usually use the one breath cycle, but this does not mean you cannot use a two breath cycle. As long as you follow the rules, you can experience many breathing strategies by yourself.

One Breath Cycle (Figure 3-38). When you inhale, your mind leads the Qi from your nose to your tailbone; and when you exhale, it leads the Qi from the tailbone to the nose to complete the cycle.

When to Practice

According to the documents, there are three times in the day which are considered best for practice: before midnight, dawn, and after noon (between two and three o'clock). If you cannot meditate three times a day, you should meditate in the morning and evening, and skip the afternoon session.

Postures for Practice

When you practice in the morning and in the afternoon, it is recommended that you face the east to absorb the energy from the sun and to coordinate with the rotation of the Earth. For the evening session, you should face South to take advantage of the earth's magnetic field. The general rule of thumb is to face into the predominant source of energy so that it will not unbalance you as your meditation progresses.

When you meditate, you should sit with your legs crossed on a mat or cushion about three inches thick. Your tongue should touch the roof of your mouth to connect the Yin and Yang vessels.

Once you have opened up the three gates and circulated the Qi smoothly in the Conception and Governing Vessels, you should then continue meditating to build up the Qi more strongly and to learn to store the Qi in these two reservoirs. Opening up the gates may take only a few months, but building up the Qi to an abundant level may take you many years of continued practice. At this stage, the more you practice, the more Qi you will accumulate. Remember: abundant Qi storage is the foundation of your health.

■ 3.4.2 Wai Dan Standing Still Meditation

Over the years, various Taiji and Qigong masters have created many postures for standing still meditation. Generally speaking, they are safer to practice than the Small Circulation exercises because they build up the Qi locally in parts of the body, rather than directly in the Qi vessels. The ultimate goal of this training is to combine the Qi built up by this Wai Dan practice with the Qi built up in the Lower Dan Tian through the Nei Dan practice. Advanced Taiji martial artists will do this during their standing meditation. However, as a beginner you should just do the Wai Dan training, keeping your mind calm and letting the Qi build up naturally through the postures.

We will now introduce two of the postures most commonly practiced by Taiji martial artists.

Arcing the Arms (Gong Shou, 拱手) or Embracing the Moon on the Chest (Huai Zhong Bao Yue, 懷中抱月)

Stand with one leg rooted on the ground, and the other in front of it with only the toes touching the ground. Both arms are held in front of the chest, forming a horizontal circle, with the fingertips almost touching (Figure 3-39). The tongue should touch the roof of the mouth to connect the Yin and Yang Qi Vessels (Conception and Governing Vessels respectively). The mind should be calm and relaxed and concentrated on the shoulders; breathing should be deep and regular.

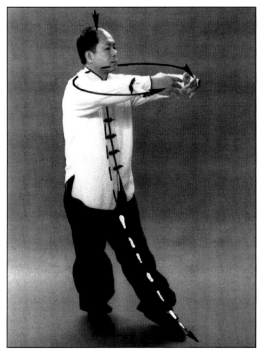

Figure 3-39

When you stand in this posture for about three minutes, your arms and one side of your back should feel sore and warm. Because the arms are held extended, the muscles and nerves are stressed. Qi will build up in this area and heat will be generated. Also, because one leg carries all the weight, the muscles and nerves in that leg and in one side of the back will be tense and will thereby build up Qi. Because this Qi is built up in the shoulders and legs rather than in the Lower Dan Tian, it is considered "local Qi" or "Wai Dan Qi" (外丹氣). In order to keep the Qi build-up and the flow in the back balanced, after three minutes change your legs without moving your arms and stand this way for another three minutes. After the six minutes, face forward, put both feet flat on the floor, shoulder-width apart, and slowly lower your arms. The accumulated Qi will then flow naturally and strongly into your arms. It is like a dam which, after accumulating a large amount of water, releases it and lets it flow. At this time, concentrate and calm the mind and look for the feeling of Qi flowing from the shoulders to the palms and fingertips. Beginners can usually sense this Qi flow, which is typically felt as warmth or a slight numbness.

Naturally, when you hold your arms out you are also slowing the blood circulation, and when you lower your arms the blood will rush down into them. This may confuse you as to whether what you feel is due to Qi or blood. You need to understand several things. First, every living blood cell has to have Qi to keep living. Thus, when you relax after the arcing hands practice, both blood and Qi will come down to the hands. Second, since blood is material and Qi is energy, Qi can flow beyond your body but your blood cannot. Therefore, it is possible for you to test whether the exercise has brought extra Qi to your hands. Place your hands right in front of your face. You should be able to feel a slight sensation, which has to come from the Qi. You can also hold your palms close to each other, or move one hand near the other arm. In addition to a slight feeling of warmth, you may also sense a kind of electric charge which may make the hairs on your arm move. These are indications of Qi's presence.

Sometimes Qi is felt on the upper lip. This is because there is a channel (Hand Yangming Large Intestine, 手陽明大腸) which runs over the top of the shoulder to the upper lip (Figure 3-40). However, the Qi feeling is usually stronger in the palms and fingers than in the lip,

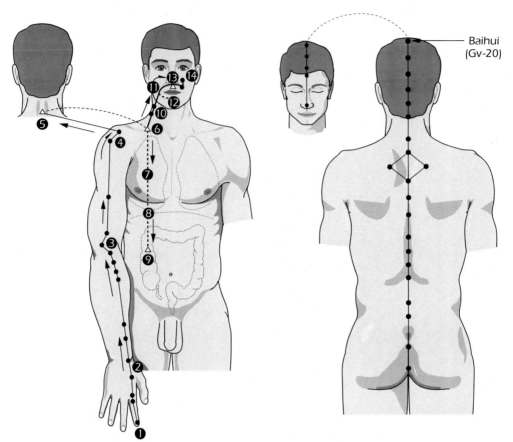

Figure 3-40. The Large Intestine Channel of Hand-Yang Brightness

Figure 3-41. The Baihui cavity

because there are six Qi channels which pass through the shoulder to end in the hand, but there is only one channel connecting the lip and shoulder. Once you experience Qi flowing in your arms and shoulders during this exercise, you may also find that you can sense it in your back.

Many advanced Taiji practitioners continue to practice this standing still meditation. In addition to building up Qi in the shoulders, they also train using the mind to lead the Qi in coordination with the breathing to complete two Qi circuits. The first Qi circuit is a horizontal one in your arms and chest. On the exhale you lead the Qi to the fingertips of both hands, and then across the gap from each hand to the other. On the inhale you lead the Qi from the fingertips to the center of your chest. The second circuit is a vertical one which connects heaven, man, and earth. On the inhale you take in Qi from nature through your Baihui (Figure 3-41) on the top of your head and lead the Qi downward to the Lower Dan Tian. On the exhale you lead the Qi further downward and out of your body through the Bubbling Well (Yongquan, K-1)(湧泉)(Figure 3-42) cavities. When you practice, the two circuits should hap-

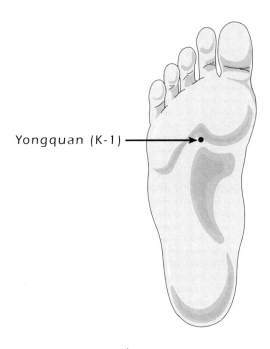

Yongquan (K-1)

Figure 3-42. The Yongquan cavity

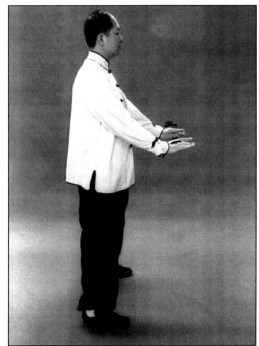

Figure 3-43

pen at the same time. If you are a beginner this is not easy to do. If you persevere, however, you will be able to use this exercise as part of your advanced practice.

This exercise is one of the most common practices for leading the beginner to experience the flow of Qi, and some Taiji styles place great emphasis on it. Similar exercises are also practiced by other styles, such as Emei Da Peng Gong (峨嵋大鵬功).

Holding Up the Heaven (Tuo Tian, 托天)

This is a very strenuous exercise, so if you are considered old or weak, you should not practice it. Instead, work with easier and more relaxed moving Qigong exercises until someday you feel strong enough to practice this one. Then make sure you start slowly and carefully.

To hold up the heaven, stand with your feet shoulder distance apart, and your arms slightly bent with the palms facing downward (Figure 3-43). Stand still, regulate your mind until it is calm and concentrated, and regulate your breathing until it is natural and smooth. Then, while inhaling, turn your hands to face each other (Figure 3-44) and lift them to shoulder height (Figure 3-45). Then, while exhaling, turn your hands palm downward (Figure 3-46) and lower your body with your palms pressing downward until both of your thighs are horizontal (Figure 3-47). Next, while inhaling, move your arms upward in front of you until the palms are facing the heavens (Figure 3-48). As you raise your hands, follow them with your eyes until you are looking upward. Finally, as you exhale raise your body slightly into the Horse

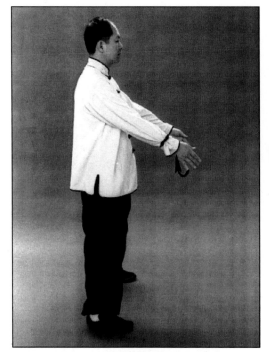

Figure 3-44

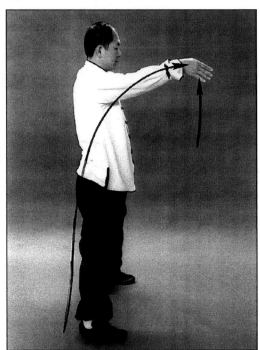

Figure 3-45

Figure 3-46

Figure 3-47

Figure 3-48

Figure 3-49

Stance (Figure 3-49). As you stand in this position, breathe regularly and keep your body as relaxed as possible.

If you are a beginner, only stay in this posture for a minute or so. As you become stronger, extend this time to three to five minutes. Always remember: your body cannot be built up in one day. Advancing slowly and safely is the key to success.

As you raise your hands to the final posture, imagine that you are lifting up the heavens, and then stand there as if you were holding up the entire sky. Keeping this idea in your mind will lead Qi from your Lower Dan Tian upward to your hands and also downward to the bottom of your feet. This exercise gradually strengthens your ankles, knees, and hips, as well as the muscles of your trunk and neck.

When you decide to stop, do not just stand up quickly. Keep your arms in position as you inhale and slowly lower your body until both thighs are horizontal (Figure 3-50). Then exhale as you lower your hands to your abdomen (Figure 3-51). Next, inhale and raise your body until you are standing upright, and at the same time lift your arms up to shoulder height with the palms facing each other (Figure 3-52). Finally, exhale and turn your palms downward as you lower them to your waist (Figure 3-53). Stand there for a few minutes and breathe deeply and regularly before moving.

To conclude this section, I would like to remind you that Nei Dan Sitting Small Circulation practice is dangerous for beginners, and you should not start it until you have

Figure 3-50

Figure 3-51

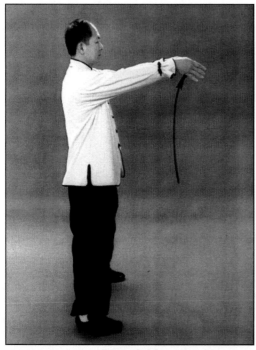

Figure 3-52

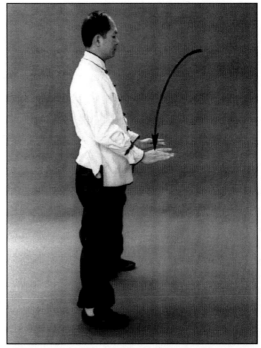

Figure 3-53

reached an advanced level. The first Wai Dan Standing Meditation presented here is generally safer for beginners, and Holding Up the Heaven is generally safe for those who are strong enough and in good health. Always remember: be cautious and proceed gradually.

3.5 Moving Taiji Qigong

Moving Taiji Qigong includes both stationary and walking exercises. In this section I will introduce three stationary sets. The first one, which I call the "primary set," is usually used for Taiji beginners. I call the second set the "coiling set," since it emphasizes coiling movements. The third set is the "rocking set." It trains the coordination of the hands, feet, and the movement of the body. These three sets actually combine the Taiji Qigong and the White Crane Qigong which I was taught, and they have benefited not only me but many of my students.

The walking set uses individual movements out of the Taiji sequence which are performed repeatedly. The criteria for performing these exercises are exactly the same as for performing the Taiji sequence. Since you are doing the same movement over and over again, you do not have to pay so much attention to the form, and can devote all of your attention to regulating your body, breathing, and mind, and to using your Yi to lead your Qi.

Before starting, you should understand that using the proper hand form is another important key to successful training. It is believed that the different hand forms originally came from imitating animals. It was found that holding the hand in the shape of the claw of an eagle, tiger, or crane led the Qi strongly to the hand. The different styles of Taijiquan have their different ways of forming the hands. It is not surprising that even within the styles some masters use different hand forms, depending upon their personal experience and understanding of Qi. I would like to introduce a hand form which I consider the best for leading Qi to the Laogong (P-8)(勞宮) cavity in the center of the palm.

In this hand form, which is called "Wa Shou" (Tile Hand, 瓦手), the hand is curved like a Chinese roof tile. The thumb and middle finger are stretched forward slightly, and the second and little fingers are pulled back slightly (Figure 3-54). After you hold this hand form for a few minutes you should notice the center of your palm getting warmer and warmer. Use this hand form whenever your palms are open.

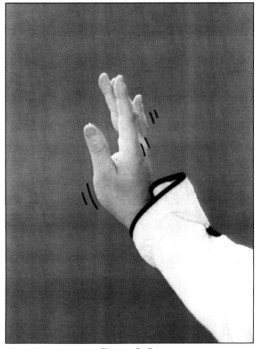

Figure 3-54

■ 3.5.1 STATIONARY TAIJI QIGONG

Primary Set

This set of Qigong exercises has several purposes:

To help the Taiji beginner understand and feel Qi. The sooner a beginner is able to understand what Qi is and to feel it, the sooner and more easily he or she can understand the internal energy of the body. This set is simple and very easy to remember, so after a short time you will be able to do it comfortably and automatically, and devote your concentration to your breathing and Qi.

To learn how to lead Qi to the limbs. When you have regulated your body, breathing, and mind, you then learn how to lead Qi from the limbs to the Lower Dan Tian when you inhale, and from the Lower Dan Tian to the limbs when you exhale. This trains you in using your Yi to lead the Qi (Yi Yi Yin Qi), which is very critical in Taiji training.

To gradually open up the twelve primary Qi channels. After you have practiced this set for a long time, you will find that the Qi is flowing more and more strongly. This stronger Qi circulation will gradually open the twelve Qi channels, and let the Qi circulate more smoothly in your twelve internal organs. This is the key to maintaining good health.

To loosen up the internal muscles. Especially those around the internal organs. This loosening removes any Qi stagnation near the internal organs, which lets them relax and receive the proper Qi nourishment.

1. **Stand Still to Regulate the Breathing (Jing Li Tiao Xi)** 靜立調息

After you have completed your warm-up Qigong, stand still and close your eyes (Figure 3-55). First pay attention to your third eye (Upper Dan Tian), and bring all of your thoughts from outside of your body to the inside. When your mind is calm and concentrated, bring your attention to your breathing. If you are doing only relaxation Qigong training, use Normal Abdominal Breathing, and if you are training for martial arts, use Reverse Abdominal Breathing. It does not matter which breathing technique you use, when you withdraw your abdomen, hold up your Huiyin cavity and anus, and when you expand your abdomen, relax or slightly expand your Huiyin cavity and anus. Remember: do not tense or strongly lift up your Huiyin cavity and anus. This will tense the lower part of your body and stagnate the Qi circulation. After you train this abdominal anus breathing for a period of time, you will feel that when you breathe, the lower part of your body is also breathing with you.

2. **Big Python Softens Its Body (Da Mang Ruan Shen)** 大蟒軟身

After you have regulated your breathing and mind, start moving your body around slowly. The motion starts at your feet, and flows upward in a wave through your legs, body, chest,

Figure 3-55

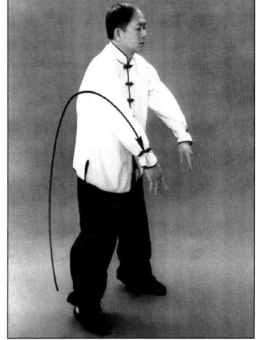

Figure 3-56

shoulder, arms, and finally reaches your fingertips (Figure 3-56). The movement feels sort of like a large snake moving around inside your body. The movement is comfortable and natural, and there is no stagnation or holding back. Do the movement for about one to two minutes, until you feel that your body is soft and comfortable from deep inside the internal organs to your limbs. After you have finished, hold your hands in front of your waist with the palms facing down (Figure 3-57). Continue to keep your mind calm, and breathe smoothly.

3. The Qi is Sunk to the Dan Tian (Qi Chen Dan Tian) 氣沉丹田

In this third exercise you are using your mind to lead the Qi to sink to the Lower Dan Tian in coordination with the movements.

Figure 3-57

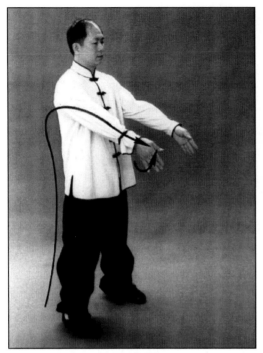

Figure 3-58

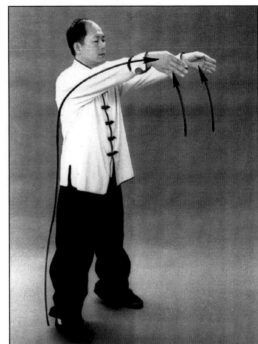

Figure 3-59

First, inhale and turn your palms towards each other (Figure 3-58) and lift them to shoulder height (Figure 3-59). Then turn both palms downward (Figure 3-60) and lower them to waist level while exhaling (Figure 3-61). Do ten repetitions, and each time you lower your hands imagine that you are pressing something down, and use the mind to lead the Qi to the Lower Dan Tian. Remember, even though it looks like you are moving only your hands, with practice you will be able to generate the movement from your legs or waist.

4. Expand the Chest to Clean the Body (Zhan Xiong Jing Shen) 展胸淨身

After you have completed the last exercise, start circling your arms up in front of you and out to the sides. As they rise in front of your chest they cross (Figure 3-62), then separate up and out to the sides (Figure 3-63). Inhale deeply as they rise, and exhale as they sink out and to the sides. The Yi and the movement start at the waist and are passed to the limbs. The chest area is especially important in this exercise. The deep breathing and the movement of the arms loosen the muscles around the lungs. While doing this exercise you should also visualize that you are expelling the dirty Qi and air from your body and lungs, and pushing them away from your body. Repeat the movements ten times.

Figure 3-60

Figure 3-61

Figure 3-62

Figure 3-63

Figure 3-64

Figure 3-65

5. Pour the Qi into the Baihui
(Baihui Guan Qi) 百會貫氣

After you have cleaned your body, you now visualize that you are taking in Qi from the heavens through your Baihui and pushing it down through your chest to the Lower Dan Tian and finally through the bottoms of your feet into the ground. The motion of this exercise is simply the reverse of the previous one. Again, the relaxation of the chest is very important. When you inhale, open your arms out in front of your abdomen (Figure 3-64), and circle them up until they are above your head (Figure 3-65). As you exhale, lower your hands palms down in front of your body while visualizing that you are pushing the Qi downward until it is below your feet (Figure 3-66). Repeat the movement ten times.

Figure 3-66

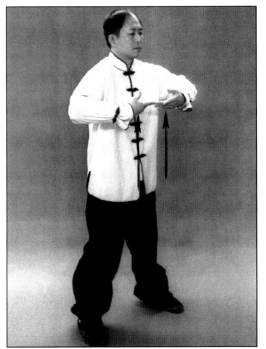

Figure 3-67

Figure 3-68

6. Left and Right to Push the Mountains (Zuo You Tui Shan)
左右推山

After you have cleaned your body and absorbed Qi from heaven, you start building Qi internally and using it for training. As you inhale, raise your hands to chest height (Figure 3-67). Lower your elbows and turn your hands until the fingers are pointing to the sides and the palms are facing down (Figure 3-68). Keep your wrists loose. As you exhale, extend your arms to the sides. When the arms are halfway extended, settle (lower) your wrists and push sideways with the palms as if you were pushing two mountains away (Figure 3-69). Inhale and bring your hands back with the palms facing inward (Figure 3-70), then exhale and lower the hands in front of you with the palms

Figure 3-69

Figure 3-70

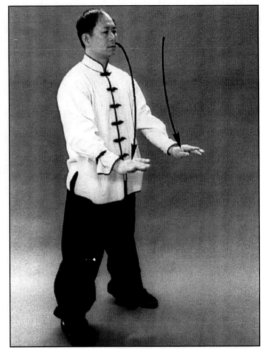

Figure 3-71

down and the fingers pointing forward (Figure 3-71). The muscles should remain relaxed throughout the exercise. Do not extend your arms to the sides as far as they can go, because this causes muscle tension and Qi stagnation. Repeat the movement ten times.

7. Settle the Wrists and Push the Palms (Zuo Wan Tui Zhang) 坐腕推掌

This exercise continues the training of using your Yi to lead your Qi, only now you are pushing forward instead of to the sides. In order to lead the Qi forward to your palms, pretend that you are pushing a car or some other heavy object. Start by raising your arms in front of you while inhaling, as you did in the previous exercise (Figure 3-72). Then lower your elbows and turn your palms forward and downward (Figure 3-73).

Figure 3-72

Figure 3-73

Figure 3-74

The wrists are relaxed and the fingers are pointing forward. Exhale and extend your arms. When they are more than halfway out, settle (lower) the wrists and push the palms forward (Figure 3-74). Do not extend your arms all the way, because that would tense the muscles and cause stagnation of the Qi circulation. Next, inhale and draw your hands back, with the palms facing your chest (Figure 3-75), and then exhale and lower your hands to your abdomen (Figure 3-76). Repeat the movement ten times.

Figure 3-75

Figure 3-76

Figure 3-77

8. Large Bear Swimming in the Water (Da Xiong You Shui)
大熊游水

When you have finished the last exercise and your hands are in front of your abdomen, raise them again while inhaling (Figure 3-77), then exhale and extend your arms forward with the palms up (Figure 3-78). Inhale and move your arms out and to the sides, turning the palms down, then circle the hands to your waist as you rotate the palms upward (Figures 3-79 and 3-80). Continue by exhaling and extending your arms forward. The motion is similar to the breast stroke in swimming. As always in Taiji, the movement is generated from the legs and directed upward to the hands. Repeat the movement ten times.

Figure 3-78

Figure 3-79

Figure 3-80

9. Left and Right to Open the Mountain (Zuo You Kai Shan) 左右開山

This is similar to the last exercise, but you use only one arm at a time. Extend your right arm while exhaling (Figure 3-81), then inhale and turn the palm down as you move it out and to the side (Figure 3-82) and then circle it down to your waist as you rotate the palm upward (Figure 3-83). When the right hand reaches your waist, do the same movement with the left hand. Do ten repetitions of the complete movement. Let your chest open and close in coordination with the arm movement, and also turn your body slightly.

Figure 3-81

Figure 3-82

Figure 3-83

10. Eagle Attacks its Prey (Lao Ying Pu Shi) 老鷹撲食

This exercise uses the reverse of the movement of the eighth exercise. Starting with your hands at your waist, inhale and spread your arms out to the sides (Figure 3-84), then exhale as your arms circle out and forward with the palms facing down (Figure 3-85). Finally, pull your hands back to your waist as the palms rotate upward (Figure 3-86). Exhale as your arms move forward, and inhale as they move back. Again, the motion originates with the legs. Repeat ten times.

Figure 3-84

Figure 3-85

Figure 3-86

11. Lion Rotates the Ball (Shi Zi Gong Qiu) 獅子拱球

This exercise is similar to the preceding one, except that you use only one arm at a time. Starting with your hands at your waist (Figure 3-87) extend your right arm to the side and then forward in a counterclockwise movement, turning the palm down as it moves (Figure 3-88). Then inhale and draw your arm back to your waist, rotating the palm upward (Figure 3-89). Then repeat the same motion with the left hand, moving it in a clockwise circle. The movement is generated by the legs, and you can vary the size

Figure 3-87

99

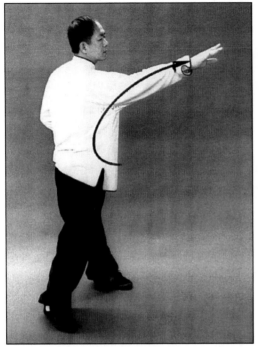

Figure 3-88

Figure 3-89

of the circles. The most important point of the training is feeling that your body is connected together from the bottom of your feet to the tips of your fingers. Repeat the complete movement ten times.

12. White Crane Spreads Its Wing (Bai He Liang Qi) 白鶴亮翅

This last form is used for recovery. In it the arms expand diagonally. When this motion is done in coordination with the breathing, the internal organs will relax and loosen, and any Qi which may still be stagnant internally will be led to the surface of your body. Continuing from the previous exercise, cross both arms in front of your chest (Figure 3-90), then exhale and extend your arms out diagonally, with the right arm up and left arm down (Figure 3-91). Inhale as

Figure 3-90

Figure 3-91

Figure 3-92

you draw both arms in and cross them in front of your chest, then exhale and extend them out diagonally again, now with the left hand up and the right hand down. The mind should remain calm and the entire body should be loose. Repeat the entire movement ten times. When you are finished, inhale and move both hands to in front of your chest (Figure 3-92), then turn both palms down (Figure 3-93). Exhale and lower your hands with the feeling that you are pushing something down, and lead the Qi back to your Lower Dan Tian (Figure 3-94). Finally, drop both hands naturally to your sides (Figure 3-95). Inhale and exhale naturally ten times and feel the Qi distributing itself in your body, especially in your hands.

Because you have been standing still for a while, your circulation may have become

Figure 3-93

Figure 3-94

Figure 3-95

Figure 3-96

Figure 3-97

stagnant and Qi and blood may have accumulated in your feet. You will notice this as a sensation of heat in your feet. Before you move, release the stagnation by rocking back on your heels and raising the front of your feet as you exhale (Figure 3-96), and then rocking forward onto your toes while inhaling (Figure 3-97). Repeat ten times before you start moving around.

Coiling Set

The main purpose of this set is to lead Qi to the surface of the skin and into the bone marrow through the use of breathing and the coiling motion. The principle behind this set is that when a muscle is twisted in one direction and then brought back to its starting position, the muscle is tensed and then relaxed. This continuous coiling motion causes the Qi in the primary Qi channels to be led outward to the surface of the skin and also to be condensed into the bone marrow. This strengthens the Qi which protects your body from negative outside influences, and also keeps the marrow functioning properly.

This coiling set is designed for those who wish to strengthen their Guardian Qi (Wei Qi, 衛氣) and to increase the sensitivity of their "Skin Listening" Jin, which is required for Taiji Pushing Hands. You can see that reverse breathing would be more effective than regular breathing in this set, because you can use the exhale to help lead Qi to the skin, and the inhale to help lead Qi to the marrow.

Even though this set was originally designed for martial arts Qi training, it is also a very effective health exercise. An abundant supply of Qi to the bone marrow is the key to health and longevity.

The most important key to this training is concentration. It is the mind which leads Qi to the skin and to the bone marrow in coordination with the coiling motion, so once you are familiar with the movements you should practice leading your mind into a deeper meditative state which allows you to feel or sense the Qi deep in the bones. Every coiling motion should be generated from the legs and directed to the limbs. The entire body should be soft like a whip. The motion is continuous and without stagnation, like the movement of an octopus. Naturally, breathing (which is the strategy of Qigong training) is another key to success. Your breathing should be slow, deep, and long, and you should not hold your breath. An additional key to successful training is the coordination of the anus and the Huiyin cavity, which will help your mind to lead your Qi more efficiently.

1. **Stand Calmly to Regulate the Xin and Breathing (Jing Tiao Xin Xi)** 靜調心息

Stand still, with your legs shoulder-width apart and your arms dropped naturally at your sides (Figure 3-98). Both your physical and your mental bodies are relaxed, centered, and balanced. The mind is calm and peaceful. Inhale and exhale smoothly and naturally about ten times in coordination with the holding up and relaxing of your anus and Huiyin cavity.

Figure 3-98

Figure 3-99

2. White Crane Relaxes Its Wings (Bai He Dou Chi) 白鶴抖翅

Inhale and turn your palms to the rear while rounding the shoulders forward and slightly arcing in your chest (Figure 3-99). As you inhale, hold up your anus and Huiyin cavity. Next, exhale as you turn your palms forward. As you do this, draw your shoulders back and relax your anus and Huiyin cavity (Figure 3-100). Remember, in all of these movements both the Yi and the actual action begin in the feet, pass through the chest, and finally reach the fingertips. Repeat the movement ten times.

Figure 3-100

Figure 3-101

Figure 3-102

3. Drill Forward and Pull Back (Qian Zuan Hou Ba) 前鑽後拔

Inhale and lift your hands up to mid-chest height. Your chest should be slightly arced in, and your fingers and arms should be in a straight line (Figure 3-101). Pull in the elbows and extend your arms in front of you, palm up, as you exhale and gently round your shoulders forward (Figure 3-102). Inhale as you spread your elbows out to the sides and draw your arms back to your chest. Rotate your arms as they move so that they end up with the palms facing your chest. The arms and fingers should be in a straight line (Figure 3-103). As you exhale, press your hands down while keeping them in line (Figure 3-104). Repeat the entire movement ten times.

Figure 3-103

Figure 3-104

Figure 3-105

4. Left and Right Yin and Yang (Zuo You Yin Yang) 左右陰陽

Continuing from the last exercise, once your
right hand forward and rotate the palm upward
(Figures 3-105 and 3-106). Then inhale and pull
(Figure 3-107). Then exhale and drill your left ha
exhaling and turning your body slightly (Figure
your arms lined up in front of your abdomen (F

5. Water and Fire Mutually Interact (Kan Li

Continuing from the last exercise, inhale, tu
hands to chest height as if you were lifting some
(Figure 3-112) and then push them downward
(Figure 3-113). Repeat ten times.

6. Large Bear Encircles the Moon (Da Xiong

Continuing from the last exercise, inhale ar
the palms up (Figure 3-114). As you exhale, exte

Figure 3-106

Figure 3-107

Figure 3-108

arms and chest form a large circle with the palms facing forward (Figure 3-115). As you inhale, move your hands back to in front of your chest, rotating the arms until the palms are facing upward (Figure 3-116). Finally, exhale and push both palms down to your abdomen, keeping both hands in a line (Figure 3-117). Do ten repetitions. Remember, when you raise your hands, to imagine that you are lifting something, and when you push down, to imagine that you are pushing something down. Also remember that when you extend your arms they should form a circle with your chest.

Figure 3-109

Figure 3-110

Figure 3-111

7. Living Buddha Holds Up the Heavens (Huo Fo Tuo Tian) 活佛托天

This exercise is similar to the last one, except that now you push your hands upward instead of forward. On the first inhale raise your hands to chest level (Figure 3-118), and then turn the palms upward (Figure 3-119) as you push upward and exhale (Figure 3-120). On the second inhale, rotate your palms and lower your hands to your chest (Figure 3-121), and as you exhale, push your hands palm downward to your abdomen (Figure 3-122). Repeat ten times.

Figure 3-112

Figure 3-113

Figure 3-114

Figure 3-115

Figure 3-116

Figure 3-117

Figure 3-118

8. Turn Heaven and Earth in Front of your Body (Shang Xia Qian Kun) 上下乾坤

First turn your palms upward and raise both hands to your chest while inhaling, then exhale and push up with one hand and down with the other (Figures 3-123 and 3-124). As you inhale, bring both hands to your chest (Figure 3-125), and then exhale and push up and down with the opposite hands (Figure 3-126). Repeat ten times.

9. Golden Rooster Twists Its Wings (Jin Ji Yao Qi) 錦雞拗翅

This exercise is very similar to the last one, except that the hand pushing down is behind you. As you inhale, bring both hands to your chest (Figure 3-127), and as you

Figure 3-119

Figure 3-120

Figure 3-121

exhale, separate them and push them up and down (Figure 3-128). Then inhale again and bring both hands to your chest (Figure 3-129), separate them, and push them up and down as you exhale (Figure 3-130). Repeat ten times.

10. Turn your Head to Look at the Moon
(Hui Tou Wang Yue) 回頭望月

Continue from the last exercise with the same hand motion and breath coordination, but now twist your body as you exhale (Figures 3-131 and 3-132). When you inhale, twist your body to face the front and draw both hands to in front of your chest

Figure 3-122

Figure 3-123

Figure 3-124

(Figure 3-133), and when you exhale, twist your body to the side and separate your hands (Figure 3-134). If your right hand is up you should twist to the left, and vice versa. Repeat ten times.

11. Big Python Turns Its Body (Da Mang Zhuan Shen)
大蟒轉身

After you have finished the last exercise, step your left leg to the left and squat down to place about sixty percent of your weight on it. Your body twists and your arms move

Figure 3-125

Figure 3-126

Figure 3-127

Figure 3-128

Figure 3-129

Figure 3-130

Figure 3-131

exactly as in the last exercise (Figures 3-135 and 3-136). When you twist your body to the left, also twist your head to look to your rear. Your right hand is above your head, and you are twisting your whole body from your fingertips to your feet. When you inhale, twist your body back to face forward while exchanging your hands (Figure 3-137). Finally, exhale and twist your body to the other side (Figure 3-138). Let your feet pivot as needed to keep your stance stable. Repeat the entire movement ten times.

12. Up and Down Coiling
(**Shang Xia Xuan Pan**) 上下旋盤

After you have completed the last exercise, turn your body to face forward and

Figure 3-132

Figure 3-133

Figure 3-134

place your hands at your waist (Figure 3-139). Next, exhale and stand up, and at the same time raise your arms straight up with the palms facing forward (Figures 3-140 and 3-141). Then inhale and lower your body as you twist it to the rear, and simultaneously draw your arms in to your chest with the palms facing in. You should end up in the Sitting on Crossed Legs Stance (Figures 3-142 and 3-143). Then raise and twist your body to the front into the Horse Stance (Figure 3-144), and continue to raise your hands over your head, rotating the palms outward (Figure 3-145). Your feet should pivot as needed to keep your stance stable. Repeat the same movement to the other side (Figures 3-146 to 3-148). Repeat ten times. After you finish, inhale and bring the hands down to your

Figure 3-135

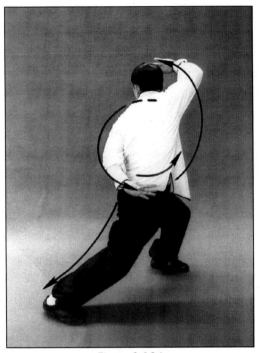

Figure 3-136

Figure 3-137

chest (Figure 3-149), and then exhale and lower them down to your waist (Figure 3-150). The entire body is like a spring, bouncing and coiling up and down slowly in coordination with the breathing. Weaker or older practitioners may find this exercise too strenuous. If this is the case, either skip it, or reduce the number of repetitions.

After you have finished the entire coiling set, stand still, and regulate your mind and breathing for a few minutes (Figure 3-151). Feel the Qi redistributing. Remain standing for a couple of minutes before you move.

Rocking Set

The rocking set was originally designed to teach the martial Taiji practitioner to bal-

Figure 3-138

Figure 3-139

Figure 3-140

Figure 3-141

Figure 3-142

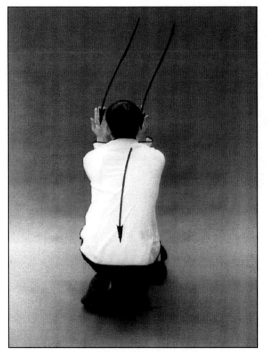

Figure 3-143

Figure 3-144

ance his Qi when doing Jin. It says in Zhang, San-Feng's Treatise: "If there is a top, there is a bottom; if there is a front, there is a back; if there is a left, there is a right. If Yi wants to go upward, this implies considering downward."[3] From this saying it is very clear that the secret of effective Jin manifestation is balanced Yi and Qi.

Analyzing this subject further, Jin balance includes first balancing the posture, which comes from firm rooting and centering. Only then will the body be comfortable and stable, and the judgment of the Yi accurate. When this Yi is used to lead the Qi to energize the muscles, you will be able to manifest your strongest Jin.

The motion of the rocking is very simple. You simply shift your weight from leg to leg in coordination with the arm move-

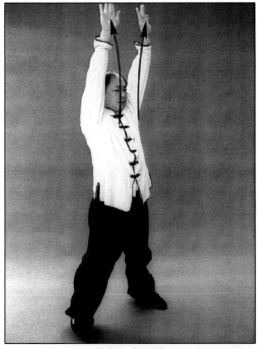

Figure 3-145

Figure 3-146

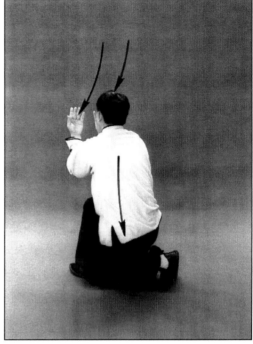

Figure 3-147

Figure 3-148

Figure 3-149

| Figure 3-150 | Figure 3-151 |

ments. When you move forward, the action of the arms is balanced by the rear leg, and when you shift your weight to the rear leg and withdraw your arms, the movement is balanced by the front leg. The repeated rocking movement helps you to develop a feeling for centering and balancing, and to build the root from which power can be grown. Although this set was originally created for Jin training, many Taiji practitioners have found that it can significantly improve leg strength and also train both physical and mental centering and balance. This also contributes to good health.

We will introduce only five exercises, but after you have practiced them for a while and understand the theory, you should be able to find or create others.

1. Embracing Arms (Gong Bi) 拱臂

Start in the Bow and Arrow Stance, with sixty percent of your weight on your front foot and both arms stretched out in front of you (Figure 3-152). Inhale and shift your weight slowly back to your rear foot until it carries sixty percent of the weight. As you shift back, lower and draw in your arms while rotating them so that the palms are facing up (Figure 3-153). Continue to circle both arms sidewards and up to shoulder height. As you raise your arms,

Figure 3-152

Figure 3-153

rotate them so that the palms are facing down when they reach shoulder height (Figure 3-154). Then exhale and move both hands forward while once again shifting sixty percent of the body's weight to the front leg (Figure 3-155). Repeat ten times, then switch your legs and repeat the same movement another ten times.

2. Wardoff (Peng) 掤

This form is adapted from the Taiji sequence. Start with your right leg forward, your right arm in front of your chest with the palm facing in, and your left hand just behind and below the right arm with the palm facing forward. The rear hand should not touch the front arm (Figure 3-156). As you shift your weight to your rear leg, inhale and move both hands down (Figure 3-157). Continuing the motion, exhale and shift your weight to the front leg while raising both arms in a wardoff movement (Figure 3-158). The motion is generated from the legs, and directed by the waist out to the right arm and left hand. Repeat the motion ten times, and then switch legs for another ten repetitions.

Figure 3-154

Figure 3-155

Figure 3-156

Figure 3-157

Figure 3-158

Figure 3-159

3. Rollback and Press (Lu Ji) 攦擠

This movement is also adapted from the Taiji form. Start in the right Bow and Arrow Stance with your right arm in front of your chest and your left hand behind the right wrist (Figure 3-159). Exhale and coil your right hand forward and upward like a snake coiling up a branch (Figures 3-160 and 3-161). Your left hand stays next to your right arm and follows its movements. As you inhale, smoothly continue the motion by turning your right palm down and starting the rollback movement while shifting your weight to the rear leg until you are in the Four-Six Stance and your body is turned slightly to the left (Figure 3-162). Move your left arm through a small circle (Figure 3-163), and then touch your left hand to

Figure 3-160

Figure 3-161

Figure 3-162

your right wrist (Figure 3-164). Finally, exhale and use the left hand to press the right wrist forward as you shift sixty percent of your weight to the front leg (Figure 3-165). After you have finished ten repetitions, switch your legs and do ten repetitions on the other side.

4.   Push (An) 按

This movement is also adapted from the Taiji sequence. Start by pushing forward with both hands while in the Bow and Arrow Stance (Figure 3-166). As you inhale, shift your weight to your rear leg into the

Figure 3-163

Figure 3-164

Figure 3-165

Four-Six Stance, and simultaneously raise your hands up and then draw them back to your chest (Figures 3-167 and 3-168). As you exhale, push your hands forward while once again shifting your weight forward into the Bow and Arrow Stance (Figure 3-169). When you push you should remain relaxed, but you should really feel that you are pushing a heavy object. Always remember that you must push your rear leg backward in order to obtain forward pushing power. Repeat ten times on each leg.

5. Rotating the Ball (Zhuan Qiu)
轉球

Rotating the ball teaches the Taiji practitioner how to relax and soften the waist and chest, and also how to use the waist to direct the movements of the arms and

Figure 3-166

Figure 3-167

Figure 3-168

hands. There is no specific pattern of movements in this exercise. You simply hold your arms in front of your chest with the palms facing each other as if you were holding a basketball, and then rotate the ball around in various ways and also move it up, down, and to the sides. You can turn your body in various directions, raise and lower it, and shift forward and backward (Figures 3-170 and 3-171). Generate the movement from your legs and direct it with your waist. You may rotate the ball any way you want as long as your palms remain facing each other and stay the same distance apart. Practice three minutes with the right leg forward and then change legs and practice for another three minutes.

You may have noticed that these exercises all work to develop the connection from

Figure 3-169

Figure 3-170

Figure 3-171

the rooted legs to the waist, chest, shoulders, and finally to the hands. This is the most essential requirement in Taiji practice. In order to reach this goal your body must be very soft, and the movement from the legs to the hands must be continuous and fluid. This builds a firm foundation for moving Taijiquan and also for manifesting Jin.

■ 3.5.2 Walking Taiji Qigong

Walking Taiji Qigong is essentially Taijiquan itself. Most of the walking movements are adapted from the Taiji sequence, the only difference being that a single movement is repeated continuously until you can feel the movement of Qi. Since you are only doing one basic movement, it is easy to remember and master, and you can put all your attention on being relaxed, centered, and balanced, and thereby regulate your body. Then you can start regulating your breathing and mind, which is the key to leading your Qi. Walking Taiji Qigong should be trained before the beginner starts learning the Taiji sequence. Experienced practitioners often practice walking Taiji Qigong to penetrate to a deeper understanding of Qi, the mind, and the body.

1. **Wave Hands in Clouds (Yun Shou)** 雲手

Squat down into Horse Stance with your hands at waist height (Figure 3-172). Inhale and

| Figure 3-172 | Figure 3-173 |

circle your right hand to in front of your left hand (Figure 3-173) and upward to chest level (Figure 3-174). Keeping your weight in the center, exhale and turn your body to the right. The hands naturally follow the turn of the body (Figure 3-175). Once your body is turned, inhale and press your right hand down and lift your left arm up to chest height while moving your left leg to the side of the right leg (Figure 3-176). Then exhale and turn your body to the left, letting your hands follow naturally (Figure 3-177). Continue by stepping your right leg to the right as you switch your hands, and then turn to the right as you start shifting your weight to the right leg. Feel the center like a cylinder running straight up the inside of your body. Repeat as many times as you wish. The arms should be very light, and should float around like clouds. The main purpose of this exercise is to loosen the waist and spine, and also to learn how to direct the power from the legs to the hands with a rotating motion.

2. Diagonal Flying (Xie Fei Shi) 斜飛勢

Start in the Bow and Arrow Stance with your left hand in front of your face and your right hand out to your side at lower chest height (Figure 3-178). As you inhale, rotate your body slightly to the left. As you turn, rotate your left arm so that the palm is facing down, pull your right arm in and rotate it so that the hand is palm up under the left hand, and also pull in your right leg next to your left leg (Figure 3-179). Step your right leg out to the right front. As you exhale, shift sixty percent of your weight forward onto your right leg, rotate your body toward the right leg, and separate your arms (Figure 3-180). The movement of the right arm is pow-

Figure 3-174

Figure 3-175

Figure 3-176

Figure 3-177

Figure 3-178   Figure 3-179

ered by the rotation of the body. The right arm should not go out past the side of the body. Next, inhale and rotate your body slightly to your right. At the same time, rotate your right arm so the palm faces down, draw in the left arm and rotate it so that the hand is palm up under the right hand, and draw in your left leg (Figure 3-181). Step your left leg out to your left front, then exhale and shift your body forward. At the same time, rotate your body toward the left leg and separate your arms so that you end up in the position from which you started. While practicing this movement you should arc in your chest as you inhale, and expand it as you exhale. This exercise is very useful for regulating the Qi in the lungs and kidneys.

3. Twist Body and Circle Fists (Pie Shen Chui) 撇身捶

Step your right leg forward and touch the heel down, and at the same time move your right arm across your body (Figure 3-182). As you exhale, shift your weight forward and twist your body so that your foot turns to the right front and your right arm circles clockwise in front of your chest (Figure 3-183). Your left arm moves with your body. Inhale and step your left leg forward and touch the heel down, and at the same time start lowering your right arm and moving your left arm across your body. Then exhale and rotate your body to the left so that your left foot turns to the left front and your left arm circles counterclockwise up and to your left (Figure 3-184). Your right arm moves with your body. Remember that the waist always directs

Figure 3-180

Figure 3-181

Figure 3-182

Figure 3-183

Figure 3-184   Figure 3-185

the movement of the arms. Practice at least ten times.

4. Stepping Leg (Cai Tui) 踩腿

Stepping leg is used to train balance and also to strengthen the knees. Inhale and step your left leg forward with the toes facing about thirty degrees to the left (Figure 3-185). Shift your weight to the left leg and at the same time slowly kick out with your right heel while pushing your left hand forward and exhaling (Figure 3-186). Inhale and step your right leg forward with the toes pointing about thirty degrees to the right (Figure 3-187), and then exhale and slowly kick the left leg out while pushing the right hand forward (Figure 3-188). While you are pushing one hand out, the other should pull back to your waist with the palm facing upward. Practice ten times.

5. Brush Knee and Step Forward (Lou Xi Yao Bu) 摟膝拗步

Stand in the Bow and Arrow Stance with the right leg forward, your right hand at your waist, and your left hand pushing forward (Figure 3-189). Inhale and start to circle your right

Figure 3-186

Figure 3-187

arm clockwise across your chest (Figure 3-190). As you exhale, rotate your body to the right, pivot your right foot to the right front corner, and push your left hand to your right. As you do this you are also shifting your weight to your front leg, and your right hand continues to circle down and to your right (Figure 3-191). Still exhaling, lift your left knee to waist height, circle your left arm down to brush past your knee, and circle your right arm back and up to by your right ear (Figure 3-192). Inhale and step your left leg forward (Figure 3-193). As you exhale, shift your weight forward, rotate your body to the front, push forward with your right hand, and draw your left arm back and down (Figure 3-194). Then repeat the entire

Figure 3-188

Figure 3-189

Figure 3-190

Figure 3-191

Figure 3-192

| Figure 3-193 | Figure 3-194 |

sequence to the other side. Practice ten repetitions.

6. Repulse Monkey (Dao Nian Hou) 倒撵猴

Start in the Four-Six Stance with your right leg forward, your right hand pushing forward, and your left hand at your waist (Figure 3-195). Next, inhale and rotate your right arm so the palm faces up, and at the same time circle your left hand back and up to behind your left ear while lifting your right leg up (Figure 3-196). Use the momentum of lifting your right leg to rotate your body and pivot on your left foot so that the toes face forward. Your left hand should reach the vicinity of your ear about this time (Figure 3-197). Then step your right leg back, exhale and shift your weight to the right leg, and at the same time push your left hand forward while withdrawing your right hand back to your waist (Figure 3-198). Continue the same movement with the other leg and keep stepping backward ten times.

7. Snake Creeps Down
(She Shen Xia Shi) 蛇身下勢 and Golden Rooster Stands on
One Leg (Jin Ji Du Li) 金雞獨立

Start in the Bow and Arrow Stance with the left palm pushing forward and the right hand raised behind you (the Single Whip posture)(Figure 3-199). As you inhale, shift your weight

Figure 3-195

Figure 3-196

Figure 3-197

Figure 3-198

Figure 3-199

Figure 3-200

back to the right leg, squat down, and withdraw your left hand back to your chest (Figure 3-200). Circle your left hand down and move it along your left leg (Figure 3-201). Start to exhale, turn your left foot thirty degrees to the side while shifting your weight onto it. As your weight comes forward, first bend your knee and then straighten it partially. Your right hand rises to in front of your face, your right knee rises to waist height, and your left hand moves to your left side (Figure 3-202). Finally, step your right leg forward, squat down, inhale and repeat the same movements on the other leg (Figure 3-203). Practice ten times.

When you train these walking Qigong exercises, the movements as always start from the legs, are directed by the waist, and

Figure 3-201

Figure 3-202

Figure 3-203

finally reach to the hands. Practice until the movements are smooth and natural, the breathing is calm, deep, and comfortable, and your mind is meditatively concentrated. Remember to coordinate the movement of your Huiyin cavity and anus with your breathing. This is the key to advancing from external Taiji feeling into the field of internal Taiji sensing.

References

1. 以意引氣。

2. 神息相依。

3. 張三豐：〝有上即有下，有前即有後，有左即有右，如意要向上，即寓下意。〞

Conclusion

結論

There is so much to Taiji that it is impossible to cover all of its theory and training in only a few books. It is also impossible for anyone to claim that he thoroughly understands Taiji theory and has completed the training in his short lifetime. In fact, only those advanced Taiji players who have reached the essence of the art's theory and practice will understand its real depth. It seems that the more you dig, the deeper it is, and the more you open your eyes, the further you will see. We need many experienced Taiji masters to open their minds and share what they have learned with the public. Only in this way will the study of Taijiquan reach a profound level and benefit mankind.

I have had several goals in publishing this book. First, I hope to lead interested Taiji players into the field of the inner feelings of Taijiquan. Many people who practice Taijiquan today are only looking to relax their bodies, and they still pay most of their attention to regulating the physical body. I hope that through this book they will be able to access the inner side of Taiji practice. Second, I would like to help teach those who are interested in Taiji as a martial art the correct ways of moving the body, and also how to lead Qi to the limbs. A soft body and the coordination of the mind and Qi are the key to Taiji power. Taiji Qigong training will enable them to build the foundation for martial applications. Third, to introduce Taiji Qigong to those of the general public who would like to improve their health.

I hope that this book will generate wide effects, like a stone thrown in a pond. If this book can bring health to the general public, then my dream will have come true.

Translation and Glossary of Chinese Terms

Ai 愛
Love, kindness.

An 按
Push.

An Mo 按摩
Literally, "press rub." Together they mean massage.

An Yang, Henan province 河南、安陽
The location of an old Chinese capital during the Shang dynasty (1766-1154 B.C.) It has become an important site for archeological study.

Ba Duan Jin 八段錦
Eight Pieces of Brocade. A Wai Dan Qigong practice which is said to have been created by Marshal Yue Fei during the Southern Song dynasty (1127-1279 A.D.).

Ba Kua Chang (Baguazhang) 八卦掌
Eight Trigrams Palm. One of the internal Qigong martial styles, believed to have been created by Dong, Hai-Chuan between 1866 and 1880 A.D.

Bagua (Ba Kua) 八卦
Literally, "Eight Divinations." Also called the Eight Trigrams. In Chinese philosophy, the eight basic variations; shown in the *Yi Jing* as groups of single and broken lines.

Baguazhang (Ba Kua Chang) 八卦掌
Eight Trigrams Palm. One of the internal Qigong martial styles, believed to have been created by Dong, Hai-Chuan between 1866 and 1880 A.D.

Bai He 白鶴
Means "White Crane." One of the Chinese southern martial styles.

Baihui (Gv-20) 百會
Literally, "hundred meetings." An important acupuncture cavity located on the top of the head. The Baihui cavity belongs to the Governing Vessel.

Bao Pu Zi 抱朴子
The Name of a well known Qigong and Chinese medical book written by Ge Hong during the Jin dynasty in the 3rd century A.D.

Bao Shen Mi Yao 保身祕要
A Qigong and medical book which described moving and stationary Qigong practices. Written by Cao, Yuan-Bai during the Qing dynasty (1644-1911 A.D.).

Bi Gang 閉肛
Close the anus.

Bian Que 扁鵲
A well known physician who wrote the book, *Nan Jing (Classic on Disorders)* during the Chinese Qin and Han dynasties (221 B.C.-220 A.D.).

Bian Shi 砭石
Stone probes which were used to press the acupuncture cavities for healing before metal needles were available.

Cao, Yuan-Bai 曹元白
A well known physician and Qigong master who wrote a book called *Bao Shen Mi Yao (The Secret Important Document of Body Protection)*, which described moving and stationary Qigong practices, during Qing dynasty (1644-1911 A.D.).

Chan (Ren) 禪，忍
A Chinese school of Mahayana Buddhism which asserts that enlightenment can be attained through meditation, self-contemplation and intuition, rather than through study of scripture. Chan is called Ren in Japan.

Chang 長
Long.

Chang Chuan (Changquan) 長拳
Means "Long Range Fist." Chang Chuan includes all northern Chinese long range martial styles. Chang Chuan has also been used to refer to Taijiquan.

Changqiang (Gv-1) 長強
Longstrength. Name of a cavity in the Governing Vessel, located in the tailbone area.

Changquan (Chang Chuan) 長拳
Means "Long Range Fist." Changquan includes all northern Chinese long range martial styles. Chang Chuan has also been used to refer to Taijiquan.

Chao, Yuan-Fang 巢元方
A well known physician and Qigong master during the Sui and Tang dynasties (581-907 A.D.). Chao, Yuan-Fang compiled the Zhu Bing Yuan Hou Lun (Thesis on the Origins and Symptoms of Various Diseases), which is a veritable encyclopedia of Qigong methods, listing 260 different ways to increase Qi flow.

Chen, Ji-Ru 陳繼儒
A well known physician and Qigong master who wrote the book, *Yang Shen Fu Yu (Brief Introduction to Nourishing the Body)* about the three treasures: Jing (essence), Qi (internal energy), and Shen (spirit) during the Qing dynasty (1644-1911 A.D.).

Chen Jia Gou 陳家溝
Chen Village. Name of the village of the Chen family, where Chen Style Taijiquan originated.

Cheng, Gin-Gsao 曾金灶
Dr. Yang, Jwing-Ming's White Crane master.

Chi (Qi) 氣
The energy pervading the universe, including the energy circulating in the human body.

Chi Kung (Qigong) 氣功
The Gongfu of Qi, which means the study of Qi.

Chin Na (Qin Na) 擒拿
Literally means "grab control." A component of Chinese martial arts which emphasizes grabbing techniques, to control your opponent's joints, in conjunction with attacking certain acupuncture cavities.

Chun Qiu 春秋
Spring and Autumn Period. One of the Chinese warring periods (722-484 B.C.).

Confucius 孔子
A Chinese scholar, during the period of 551-479 B.C., whose philosophy has significantly influenced Chinese culture.

Da Jin 打勁
Striking Jin. The power of striking.

Da Mo 達摩
The Indian Buddhist monk who is credited with creating the Yi Jin Jing and Xi Sui Jing while at the Shaolin monastery. His last name was Chadili and he was also known as Bodhidarma. He was once the prince of a small tribe in southern India.

Da Qiao 搭橋
To build a bridge. Refers to the Qigong practice of touching the roof of the mouth with the tip of the tongue to form a bridge or link between the Governing and Conception Vessels.

Da Zhou Tian 大周天
Literally, "Grand Cycle Heaven." Usually translated Grand Circulation. After a Nei Dan Qigong practitioner completes Small Circulation, he will circulate his Qi through the entire body or exchange the Qi with nature.

Dan Tian 丹田
Literally, "Field of Elixir." Locations in the body which are able to store and generate Qi (elixir) in the body. The Upper, Middle, and Lower Dan Tian are located respectively between the eyebrows, at the solar plexus, and a few inches below the navel.

Dan Tian Qi 丹田氣
Usually, the Qi which is converted from Original Essence and is stored in the Lower Dan Tian. This Qi is considered "water Qi" and is able to calm down the body. Also called Xian Tian Qi (Pre-Heaven Qi).

Dao 道
The "way," by implication the "natural way."

Dao De Jing 道德經
Morality Classic. Written by Lao Zi.

Dao Jia 道家
The Dao family; Daoism. Created by Lao Zi during the Zhou dynasty (1122-934 B.C.). In the Han dynasty (c. 58 A.D.), it was mixed with the Buddhism to become the Daoist religion (Dao Jiao).

Dao Jiao 道教
Dao religion created by Zhang, Dao-Ling, who combined the traditional Daoist principles with Buddhism during Chinese Han dynasty.

Di 地
The Earth. Earth, Heaven (Tian) and Man (Ren) are the "Three Natural Powers" (San Cai).

Di Li Shi 地理師
Di Li means "geomancy" and Shi means "teacher." Therefore Di Li Shi is a teacher or master who analyzes geographic locations according to the formulas in the *Yi Jing (Book of Changes)* and the energy distributions in the Earth. Also called Feng Shui Shi.

Di Qi 地氣
The Qi or the energy of the earth.

Dian Mai (Dim Mak) 點脈
Mai means "the blood vessel" (Xue Mai) or "the Qi channel" (Qi Mai). Dian Mai means "to press the blood vessel or Qi channel."

Dian Xue 點穴
Dian means "to point and exert pressure" and Xue means "the cavities." Dian Xue refers to those Qin Na techniques which specialize in attacking acupuncture cavities to immobilize or kill an opponent.

Dian Xue massages 點穴按摩
One of Chinese massage techniques in which the acupuncture cavities are stimulated through pressing. Dian Xue massage is also called acupressure and is the root of Japanese Shiatsu.

Dim Mak (Dian Mai) 點脈
Cantonese of "Dian Mai."

Dong, Hai-Chuan 董海川
A well known Chinese internal martial artist who is credited as the creator of Baguazhang in the late Qing dynasty (1644-1911 A.D.).

Du Mai 督脈
Usually translated "Governing Vessel." One of the eight extraordinary vessels.

Eastern Han dynasty 東漢
A Chinese dynasty during the period from 25-168 A.D.

Emei 峨嵋
Name of a mountain in Sichuan Province, China.

Emei Da Peng Gong 峨嵋大鵬功
Da Peng is a kind of large bird which existed in ancient China. Da Peng Gong is a style of Qigong which imitates the movements of this bird. This style was developed at Emei mountain in China.

Fa Jin 發勁
Emitting Jin. The power which is usually used for an attack.

Fan Fu Hu Xi 反腹呼吸
Reverse abdominal breathing. One of the Qigong breathing methods. Also called "Fan Hu Xi" (reverse breathing) or "Daoist breathing."

Fan Hu Xi 反呼吸
Reverse breathing. Also commonly called "Daoist Breathing."

Fan Jing Bu Nao 返精補腦
A special Daoist Qigong terminology which means "to return the Jing to nourish the brain."

Fan Tong 返童
Back to childhood. A training in Nei Dan Qigong through which the practitioner tries to regain control of the muscles of the lower abdomen.

Fan Tong Hu Xi 返童呼吸

Back to childhood breathing. A breathing training in Nei Dan Qigong through which the practitioner tries to regain control of the muscles in the lower abdomen. Also called "abdominal breathing."

Feng Shui Shi 風水師

Literally, "wind water teacher." Teacher or master of geomancy. Geomancy is the art or science of analyzing the natural energy relationships in a location, especially the interrelationships between "wind" and "water," hence the name. Also called Di Li Shi.

Fu Shi Hu Xi 腹式呼吸

Literally, "abdominal way of breathing." As you breathe, you use the muscles in the lower abdominal area to control the diaphragm. It is also called "back to (the) childhood breathing."

Ge Hong 葛洪

A famous physician and Qigong master who wrote the book, *Bao Pu Zi* during Jin dynasty in the 3rd century A.D.

Ge Zhi Yu Lun 格致餘論

Chinese name of the book, *A Further Thesis of Complete Study.* A medical and Qigong thesis written by Zhu, Dan-Xi during the Chinese Song, Jin, and Yuan dynasties (960-1368 A.D.).

Gong Bi 拱臂

Arc the arms. A common Taiji Qigong practice.

Gong Shou 拱手

Arcing the arms or hands. A stationary Taiji Qigong training.

Gongfu (Kung Fu) 功夫

Means "energy-time." Anything which will take time and energy to learn or to accomplish is called Gongfu.

Gui Qi 鬼氣

The Qi residue of a dead person. It is believed by the Chinese Buddhists and Daoists that this Qi residue is a so called ghost.

Guoshu (Kuoshu) 國術

Abbreviation of "Zhongguo Wushu," which means "Chinese Martial Techniques."

Han dynasty 漢朝

A dynasty in Chinese history (206 B.C.-221 A.D.).

Han, Ching-Tang 韓慶堂

A well known Chinese martial artist, especially in Taiwan in the last forty years. Master Han is also Dr. Yang, Jwing-Ming's Long Fist Grand Master.

He 和

Harmony or peace.

Hebei province 河北

One of the Chinese provinces to the north of the Yellow River.

Henan 河南

One of the Chinese provinces on the south of the Yellow River.

Hou Tian Qi 後天氣

Post-Birth Qi. This Qi is converted from the Essence of food and air and is classified as "fire Qi" since it can make your body too Yang.

Hsing Yi Chuan (Xingyiquan) 形意拳
Literally, Shape-mind Fist. An internal style of Gongfu in which the mind or thinking determines the shape or movement of the body. Creation of the style attributed to Marshal Yue Fei.

Hu Bu Gong 虎步功
Tiger Step Gong. A style of Qigong training.

Hua Jin 化勁
Neutralizing Jin. A special Taiji power training which allows you to neutralize incoming force.

Hua Tuo 華陀
A well known physician during the Chinese Jin dynasty in the 3rd century A.D.

Huan 緩
Slow.

Huiyin (Co-1) 會陰
An acupuncture cavity which belongs to the Conception Vessel.

Huo Long Gong 火龍功
Fire Dragon Gong. A style of Qigong training created by Taiyang martial stylists.

Jiaji 夾脊
Squeeze the spine. A cavity name used by Qigong practitioners. The acupuncture name of the same cavity is Lingtai (Gv-10). See also Lingtai.

Jia Gu Wen 甲骨文
Oracle-Bone Scripture. Earliest evidence of the Chinese use of the written word. Found on pieces of turtle shell and animal bone from the Shang dynasty (1766-1154 B.C.). Most of the information recorded was of a religious nature.

Jiao Hua Gong 叫化功
Beggar Gong. A style of Qigong training.

Jin 勁
A power in Chinese martial arts which is derived from muscles which have been energized by Qi to their maximum potential.

Jin 金
A dynasty in Chinese history (1115-1234 A.D.).

Jin dynasty 晉
A Chinese dynasty in the 3rd century A.D.

Jin Kui Yao Lue 金匱要略
A Chinese book, *Prescriptions from the Golden Chamber,* which discusses the use of breathing and acupuncture to maintain good Qi flow. This book was written by Zhang, Zhong-Jing during the Chinese Qin and Han dynasties (221 B.C.-220 A.D.).

Jin Zhong Zhao 金鐘罩
Literally, "golden bell cover." A higher level of Iron Shirt training.

Jin, Shao-Feng 金紹峰
Dr. Yang, Jwing-Ming's White Crane grand master.

Jing 精
Essence. The most refined part of anything.

Jing 靜
Calm and silent.

Jing Zi 精子
Literally, "essence son." The most refined part of human essence. The sperm.

Jun Qing 君倩
A Daoist and Chinese doctor during the Chinese Jin dynasty (265-420 A.D.). Jun Qing is credited as the creator of the Five Animal Sports Qigong practice.

Kan 坎
One of the Eight Trigrams.

Kao Tao 高濤
Master Yang, Jwing-Ming's first Taijiquan master.

Kung Fu (Gongfu) 功夫
Literally, "energy-time." Any study, learning, or practice which requires a lot of patience, energy, and time to complete. Since practicing Chinese martial arts requires a great deal of time and energy, Chinese martial arts are commonly called Gongfu.

Kuoshu (Guoshu) 國術
Literally, national techniques. Another name for Chinese martial arts. First used by President Chiang, Kai-Shek in 1926 at the rounding of the Nanking Central Guoshu Institute.

Lan Shi Mi Cang 蘭室祕藏
Secret Library of the Orchid Room. Name of a Chinese medical and Qigong book written by Li Guo during the Song, Jin, and Yuan dynasties (960-1368 A.D.).

Lao Zi 老子
The creator of Daoism, also called Li Er.

Laogong (P-8) 勞宮
Cavity name. On the Pericardium Channel in the center of the palm.

Li 離
A phase of the Bagua (Eight Trigrams), Li represents fire.

Li Er 李耳
Nickname of Lao Zi. The creator of scholarly Daoism.

Li Guo 李果
A well known Chinese physician and Qigong master who wrote the book, *Lan Shi Mi Cang (Secret Library of the Orchid Room)* during the period of the Song, Jin, and Yuan dynasties (960-1368 A.D.).

Li, Mao-Ching 李茂清
Dr. Yang, Jwing-Ming's Long Fist master.

Li, Shi-Zhen (1518-1593 A.D.) 李時珍
A well known Chinese physician and Qigong master who wrote a book about the eight Qi vessels, *Qi Jing Ba Mai Kao (Deep Study of the Extraordinary Eight Vessels)* in 16th century.

Lian Qi 練氣
Lian means "to train, to strengthen and to refine." A Daoist training process through which your Qi grows stronger and more abundant.

Liang dynasty 梁
A dynasty in Chinese history (502-557 A.D.)

Lingtai (Gv-10) 靈台
Spiritual station. An acupuncture cavity located on the Governing Vessel.

Liu He Ba Fa 六合八法
Literally, "six combinations eight methods." One of the Chinese internal martial arts, its techniques are combined from Taijiquan, Xingyiquan and Baguazhang. This internal martial art was reportedly created by Chen Bo during the Song dynasty (960-1279 A.D.).

Luo 絡
The small Qi channels which branch out from the primary Qi channels and are connected to the skin and to the bone marrow.

Mai 脈
Means "vessel" or "Qi channel."

Mencius (372-289 B.C.) 孟子
A well-known scholar who followed the philosophy of Confucius during the Chinese Zhou dynasty (909-255 B.C.).

Mian 綿
Soft.

Ming dynasty 明朝
A Chinese dynasty during the period from 1368 to 1644 A.D.

Mingmen (Gv-4) 命門
Name of an acupuncture cavity belonging to the Governing Vessel.

Nan Hua Jing 南華經
Name of a book written by the Daoist philosopher Zhuang Zi around 300 B.C. This book describes the relationship between health and the breath.

Nan Jing 難經
Classic on Disorders. A medical book written by the famous physician Bian Que during the Qin and Han dynasties (221 B.C.-220 A.D.). *Nan Jing* describes the methods of using the breathing to increase Qi circulation.

Nei Dan 內丹
Literally, "internal elixir." A form of Qigong in which Qi (the elixir) is built up in the body and spread out to the limbs.

Nei Gong 內功
Literally, "internal Gongfu." Chinese martial arts which start with internal training and the cultivation of Qi.

Nei Gong Tu Shuo 內功圖説
Illustrated Explanation of Nei Gong. Name of a Qigong book written by Wang, Zu-Yuan during Qing dynasty. This book presents the Twelve Pieces of Brocade and explains the idea of combining both moving and stationary Qigong.

Nei Jin 內勁
Internal power. The power in which Qi from the Dan Tian is used to support the muscles. This is characterized by relatively relaxed muscles. When the muscles predominate and local Qi is used to support them, it is called Wai Jin. See also Wai Jin.

Nei Jing 內經
Inner Classic. Name of a Chinese medical book written during the reign of the Yellow emperor (2690-2590 B.C.).

Ping 平
Peace and harmony.

Qi (Chi) 氣

The general definition of Qi is: universal energy, including heat, light, and electromagnetic energy. A narrower definition of Qi refers to the energy circulating in human or animal bodies. A current popular model is that the Qi circulating in the human body is bioelectric in nature.

Qi Hua Lun 氣化論

Qi variation thesis. An ancient treatise which discusses the variations of Qi in the universe.

Qi Huo 起火

To start the fire. In Qigong practice, when you start to build up Qi at the Lower Dan Tian.

Qi Jing Ba Mai 奇經八脈

Literally, "strange (odd) channels eight vessels." Usually referred to as the eight extraordinary vessels or simply as the vessels. Called odd or strange because they are not well understood and some of them do not exist in pairs.

Qi Jing Ba Mai Kao 奇經八脈考

Deep Study of the Extraordinary Eight Vessels. Name of a book written by Li, Shi-Zhen.

Qian Jin Fang 千金方

Thousand Gold Prescriptions. Name of a medical book written by a well know physician, Sun, Si-Mao, during the Sui and Tang dynasties (581-907 A.D.). This book describes the methods of leading Qi, and also describes the use of the Six Sounds.

Qiao Men 竅門

Tricky or secret door. The trick or secret can lead the practitioner to the essence of the training.

Qigong (Chi Kung) 氣功

Gong means Gongfu (lit. energy-time). Therefore, Qigong means study, research, and/or practices related to Qi.

Qigong An Mo 氣功按摩

Qigong massage.

Qihai (Co-6) 氣海

An acupuncture cavity belonging to the Conception Vessel.

Qin Na (Chin Na) 擒拿

Literally means "grab control." A component of Chinese martial arts which emphasizes grabbing techniques to control your opponent's joints, in conjunction with attacking certain acupuncture cavities.

Qing dynasty 清朝

A dynasty in Chinese history. The last Chinese dynasty (1644-1912 A.D.).

Ren 人

Man or mankind.

Ren 仁

Humanity, kindness or benevolence.

Ren Mai 任脈

Conception Vessel. One of the Eight Extraordinary Vessels.

Ren Qi 人氣

Human Qi.

Ren Zong 仁宗

One of the emperors during the Chinese Song dynasty (960-1280 A.D.). Ren Zong was in power during the period from 1023-1064 A.D.

Ru Jia 儒家

Literally, "Confucian family." Scholars following Confucian thoughts; Confucianists.

Ru Men Shi Shi 儒門視事

The Confucian Point of View. Name of a book written by Zhang, Zi-He during the Song, Jin, and Yuan dynasties (960-1368 A.D.).

Ruan Jin 軟勁

Soft Jin. Power which acts like a soft whip.

San Bao 三寶

Three treasures. Essence (Jing), energy (Qi) and spirit (Shen). Also called San Yuan (three origins).

San Cai 三才

Three powers. Heaven, Earth and Man.

San Guan 三關

Three gates. In Small Circulation training, the three cavities on the Governing Vessel which are usually obstructed and must be opened.

San Gong 散功

Literally, "energy dispersion." A state of premature degeneration of the muscles where the Qi cannot effectively energize them. It can be caused by earlier over-training.

San Shi Qi Shi 三十七勢

Thirty-seven postures. According to historical records, one of the predecessors of Taijiquan.

San Yuan 三元

Three origins. Also called "San Bao" (three treasures). Human Essence (Jing), energy (Qi) and spirit (Shen).

Shaanxi province 陝西

Chinese province.

Shang dynasty 商朝

A dynasty in Chinese history during the period from 1766-1154 B.C.

Shaolin 少林

"Young woods." Name of the Shaolin Temple.

Shaolin Temple 少林寺

A monastery located in Henan Province, China. The Shaolin Temple is well known because of its martial arts training.

Shen 神

Spirit. According to Chinese Qigong, the Shen resides at the Upper Dan Tian (the third eye).

Shen 深

Deep.

Shi Er Duan Jin 十二段錦

Twelve Pieces of Brocade, presented by Wang, Zu-Yuan in his book *Nei Gong Tu Shuo (Illustrated Explanation of Nei Gong)* during the Chinese Qing dynasty.

Shi Er Zhuang 十二庄

Twelve Postures. A style of Qigong practice created during the Chinese Qing dynasty.

Song dynasty 宋朝

A dynasty in Chinese history (960-1279 A.D.).

Song Gang 鬆肛

Relax the anus.

Song Hui Zong 宋徽宗
An emperor during the Chinese Song dynasty (960-1280 A.D.). He was in power from 1101-1126 A.D.

Southern Song dynasty 南宋
After the Song was conquered by the Jin race from Mongolia, the Song people moved to the south and established another country, called Southern Song (1127-1279 A.D.).

Suan Ming Shi 算命師
Literally, "calculate life teacher." A fortune teller who is able to calculate your future and destiny.

Sui 隨
Follow.

Sui dynasty 隋
A dynasty in China during the period of 581-618 A.D.

Sun, Si-Mao 孫思邈
A well known Chinese physician and Qigong master who wrote the book, *Qian Jin Fang (Thousand Gold Prescriptions)* during the Sui and Tang dynasties (581-907 A.D.).

Tai Chi Chuan (Taijiquan) 太極拳
A Chinese internal martial style which based on the theory of Taiji (grand ultimate).

Taiji 太極
Means "grand ultimate." It is this force which generates two poles, Yin and Yang.

Taiji Qigong 太極氣功
Qigong practice specially designed for Taijiquan practice. In this practice, a practitioner learns how to use the mind to lead the Qi.

Taijiquan (Tai Chi Chuan) 太極拳
A Chinese internal martial style which is based on the theory of Taiji (grand ultimate).

Taiyang 太陽
Greater Yang. A special term used in acupuncture.

Taizuquan 太祖拳
A style of Chinese external martial arts.

Tang dynasty 唐朝
A dynasty in Chinese history during the period 618-907 A.D.

Tao, Hong-Jing 陶弘景
A well known physician and Qigong master who compiled the book, *Yang Shen Yan Ming Lu (Records of Nourishing the Body and Extending Life)* from 420 to 581 A.D.

Tian 天
Heaven or sky. In ancient China, people believed that Heaven was the most powerful natural energy in this universe.

Tian Qi 天氣
Heaven Qi. It is now commonly used to mean the weather, since weather is governed by Heaven Qi.

Tian Chi 天池
Heavenly pond. The place under the tongue where saliva is generated.

Tiao Qi 調氣
To regulate the Qi.

Tiao Shen 調身

To regulate the body.

Tiao Shen 調神

To regulate the spirit.

Tiao Xi 調息

To regulate the breathing.

Tiao Xin 調心

To regulate the emotional mind.

Tie Bu Shan 鐵布衫

Iron shirt. Gongfu training which toughens the body externally and internally.

Tie Sha Zhang 鐵砂掌

Literally, "iron sand palm." A special martial arts conditioning for the palms.

Ting Jin 聽勁

Listening Jin. A special training in Taijiquan which uses the feeling, especially the skin's sensitivity, to ascertain the opponent's intention.

Tong Ren Yu Xue Zhen Jiu Tu 銅人俞穴鍼灸圖

Illustration of the Brass Man Acupuncture and Moxibustion. Name of an acupuncture book written by Dr. Wang, Wei-Yi during the Song dynasty.

Tui Jin 推勁

Pushing Jin. A kind of pushing power training in Taijiquan.

Tui Na 推拿

Means "to push and grab." A category of Chinese massages for healing and injury treatment.

Wa Shou 瓦手

Tile hand. The typical open-hand form used in Taijiquan.

Wai Dan 外丹

External elixir. External Qigong exercises in which a practitioner will build up the Qi in his limbs and then lead it into the center of the body for nourishment.

Wai Gong 外功

External Gongfu. Gongfu which emphasizes physical body training.

Wai Jin 外勁

External power. The type of Jin where the muscles predominate and only local Qi is used to support the muscle. See also Nei Jin.

Wai Tai Mi Yao 外台祕要

The Extra Important Secret. Name of a Chinese medical book written by Wang Tao during the Sui and Tang dynasties (581-907 A.D.). This book discusses the use of breathing and herbal therapies for disorders of Qi circulation.

Wang Tao 王燾

A well known Chinese physician and Qigong master who wrote the book *Wai Tai Mi Yao (The Extra Important Secret)* during the Sui and Tang dynasties (581-907 A.D.).

Wang, Fan-An 汪汎庵

A well known Chinese physician who wrote the book *Yi Fan Ji Jie (The Total Introduction to Medical Prescriptions)* during the Qing dynasty.

Wang, Wei-Yi 王唯一

A well known Chinese physician who wrote the book, *Tong Ren Yu Xue Zhen Jiu Tu (Illustration of the Brass Man Acupuncture and Moxibustion)* during the Song dynasty.

Wang, Zu-Yuan 王祖源
A well known Chinese physician who wrote the book, *Nei Gong Tu Shuo (Illustrated Explanation of Nei Gong)* during the Qing dynasty.

Wei Qi 衛氣
Protective Qi or Guardian Qi. The Qi at the surface of the body which generates a shield to protect the body from negative external influences such as colds.

Wei, Bo-Yang 魏伯陽
A well known physician who wrote the book, *Zhou Yi Can Tong Qi (A Comparative Study of the Zhou (dynasty) Book of Changes)* during the Qin and Han dynasties (221 B.C.-220 A.D.).

Weilu 尾閭
Tailbone. The name used by Chinese martial artists and Qigong practitioners. The acupuncture name for this cavity is Changqiang (Gv-1).

Wilson Chen 陳威伸
Dr. Yang, Jwing-Ming's friend.

Wu Qin Shi 五禽戲
Five Animal Sports. A set of medical Qigong practice created by Jun Qing during Chinese Jin dynasty (265-420 A.D.).

Wudang Mountain 武當山
Located in Fubei Province in China.

Wuji 無極
Means "no extremity."

Wuji Qigong 無極氣功
A style of Taiji Qigong practice.

Wushu 武術
Literally, "martial techniques." A common name for the Chinese martial arts. Many other terms are used, including: Wuyi (martial arts), Wugong (martial Gongfu), Guoshu (national techniques), and Gongfu (energy-time). Because Wushu has been modified in mainland China over the past forty years into gymnastic martial performance, many traditional Chinese martial artists have given up this name in order to avoid confusing modern Wushu with traditional Wushu. Recently, mainland China has attempted to bring modern Wushu back toward its traditional training and practice.

Xi 細
Slender.

Xi Sui Jing 洗髓經
Literally, "Washing Marrow/Brain Classic," usually translated "Marrow/Brain Washing Classic." A Qigong training which specializes in leading Qi to the marrow to cleanse it or to the brain to nourish the spirit for enlightenment. It is believed that Xi Sui Jing training is the key to longevity and achieving spiritual enlightenment.

Xian Tian Qi 先天氣
Pre-Birth Qi or Pre-Heaven Qi. Also called Dan Tian Qi. The Qi which is converted from Original Essence and is stored in the Lower Tian. Considered to be "water Qi," it is able to calm the body.

Xiao 孝
Filial Piety.

Xiao Jiu Tian 小九天
Small nine heaven. A Qigong style created in the sixth century.

Xiao Zhou Tian 小周天
Literally, "small heavenly cycle." Also called Small Circulation. In Qigong, when you can use your mind to lead Qi through the Conception and Governing Vessels, you have completed "Xiao Zhou Tian."

Xin 心
Means "heart." Xin means the mind generated from emotional disturbance.

Xin 信
Trust.

Xingyiquan (Hsing Yi Chuan) 形意拳
Literally, "Shape-mind Fist." An internal style of Gongfu in which the mind or thinking determines the shape or movement of the body. Creation of the style attributed to Marshal Yue Fei.

Xinzhu Xian 新竹縣
Birthplace of Dr. Yang, Jwing-Ming in Taiwan.

Xiu Qi 修氣
Cultivate the Qi. Cultivate implies to protect, maintain and refine. A Buddhist Qigong training.

Yang 陽
In Chinese philosophy, the active, positive, masculine polarity. In Chinese medicine, Yang means excessive, overactive, overheated. The Yang (or outer) organs are the Gall Bladder, Small Intestine, Large Intestine, Stomach, Bladder, and Triple Burner.

Yang Shen Fu Yu 養生膚語
Brief Introduction to Nourishing the Body. Name of a book written by Chen, Ji-Ru during the Qing dynasty.

Yang Shen Jue 養生訣
Life Nourishing Secrets. Name of a medical book written by Zhang, An-Dao during the Song, Jin, and Yuan dynasties (960-1368 A.D.).

Yang Shen Yan Ming Lu 養身延命錄
Records of Nourishing the Body and Extending Life. A Chinese medical book written by Dao, Hong-Jing in the period from 420 to 581 A.D.

Yang, Jwing-Ming 楊俊敏
Author of this book.

Yi 意
Mind. Specifically, the mind which is generated by clear thinking and judgment, and which is able to make you calm, peaceful, and wise.

Yi 義
Justice or righteousness.

Yi Fan Ji Jie 醫方集介
The Total Introduction to Medical Prescriptions. Name of a Chinese medical book written by Wang, Fan-An during the Qing dynasty.

Yi Jin Jing 易筋經
Literally, *"Changing Muscle/Tendon Classic,"* usually called *The Muscle/Tendon Changing Classic.* Credited to Da Mo around 550 A.D., this work discusses Wai Dan Qigong training for strengthening the physical body.

Yi Jing 易經
Book of Changes. A book of divination written during the Zhou dynasty (1122-255 B.C.).

Yin 陰
In Chinese philosophy, the passive, negative, feminine polarity. In Chinese medicine, Yin means deficient. The Yin (internal) organs are the Heart, Lungs, Liver, Kidneys, Spleen, and Pericardium.

Yin Jin 引勁
Leading Jin. A special power which can lead the opponent's incoming force in a desired direction.

Ying Gong 硬功
Hard Gongfu. Any Chinese martial training which emphasizes physical strength and power.

Ying Jin 硬勁
Hard Jin. A Jin which is manifested mainly through muscular power.

Ying Qi 營氣
Managing Qi. The Qi which manages the functioning of the organs and the body.

Yongquan (K-1) 湧泉
Bubbling Well. Name of an acupuncture cavity belonging to the Kidney Primary Qi Channel.

You 悠
Long, far, meditative, continuous, slow and soft.

Yuan dynasty 元代
A Chinese dynasty during the period of 1206-1367 A.D.

Yuan Jing 元精
Original Essence. The fundamental, original substance inherited from your parents, it is converted into Original Qi.

Yuan Qi 元氣
Original Qi. The Qi created from the Original Essence inherited from your parents.

Yue Fei 岳飛
A Chinese hero in the Southern Song dynasty (1127-1279 A.D.). Said to have created Ba Duan Jin, Xingyiquan and Yue's Ying Zhua.

Yun 勻
Uniform or even.

Yun Shou 雲手
Wave hands in clouds. A form in Taijiquan.

Yuzhen 玉枕
Jade pillow. One of the three gates of Small Circulation training.

Zhan Guo 戰國
Warring States Period. A period in Chinese history (403-222 B.C.).

Zhang, An-Dao 張安道
A well known Chinese physician and Qigong master who wrote the book, *Yang Shen Jue (Life Nourishing Secrets),* during the Song, Jin, and Yuan dynasties (960-1368 A.D.).

Zhang, Dao-Ling 張道陵
A Daoist who combined scholarly Daoism with Buddhist philosophies and created Religious Daoism (Dao Jiao) during the Chinese Eastern Han dynasty (25-221 A.D.).

Zhang, San-Feng 張三豐
Chang, San-Feng is credited as the creator of Taijiquan during the Song dynasty in China (960-1127 A.D.).

Zhang, Xiang-San 張詳三
A well known Chinese martial artist in Taiwan.

Zhang, Zhong-Jing 張仲景
A well known Chinese physician who wrote the book, *Jin Kui Yao Lue (Prescriptions from the Golden Chamber)*, during the Qin and Han dynasties (221 B.C.-220 A.D.).

Zhang, Zi-He 張子和
A well known Chinese physician who wrote the book, *Ru Men Shi Shi (The Confucian Point of View)*, during the Song, Jin, and Yuan dynasties (960-1368 A.D.).

Zheng Fu Hu Xi 正腹呼吸
Formal Abdominal Breathing. More commonly called Buddhist Breathing.

Zhong 忠
Loyalty.

Zhou dynasty 周朝
A dynasty in China during the period of 1122-255 B.C.

Zhou Yi Can Tong Qi 周易參同契
A medical and Qigong book written by Wei, Bo-Yang during the Qin and Han dynasties (221 B.C.-220 A.D.).

Zhu Bing Yuan Hou Lun 諸病源候論
Thesis on the Origins and Symptoms of Various Diseases. A Chinese medical book written by Chao, Yuan-Fang during the Sui and Tang dynasties (581-907 A.D.).

Zhu, Dan-Xi 朱丹溪
A well known Chinese physician who wrote the book, *Ge Zhi Yu Lun (A Further Thesis of Complete Study)*, during the Song, Jin, and Yuan dynasties (960-1368 A.D.).

Zhuan Qi Zhi Rou 專氣致柔
"Concentrate on Qi and achieve softness." A famous sentence written in Lao Zi's Dao De Jing.

Zhuan Qiu 轉球
Rotating the ball.

Zhuang Zhou 莊周
A contemporary of Mencius who advocated Daoism.

Zhuang Zi 莊子
Zhuang Zhou. A contemporary of Mencius who advocated Daoism. Zhuang Zi also means the works of Zhuang Zhou.

Zou Jin 走勁
Yielding Jin. A special power training which allows you to yield to incoming force.

Zuan Jin 鑽勁
Drilling Jin. A special kind of Taiji power which can penetrate like a drill.

INDEX

BOOKS & VIDEOS FROM YMAA

YMAA Publication Center Books

YMAA Publication Center Videotapes

YMAA PUBLICATION CENTER 楊氏東方文化出版中心

4354 Washington Street Roslindale, MA 02131
1-800-669-8892 • ymaa@aol.com • www.ymaa.com